Amazing Grace

Letters Along My Journey

Rae Lewis-Thornton
Chicago, IL

AMAZING GRACE
Published by Rae Lewis-Thornton, Inc.
1507 East 53rd Street
Suite 315
Chicago, IL 60615
www.raelewisthornton.org
(773) 643-4316

Editorial services provided by ADA Unity Publishers
14625 Baltimore Avenue, Suite 256
Laurel, MD 20707-4902
(240) 535 -0661

Editors Note: In order to maintain the original character of the letters, only minor grammatical changes were made.

Cover Design by William Flowers
P.O. Box 586
Annapolis Junction, MD 20701
uartistnet@hotmail.com
(240) 988-5621

ISBN 0-9747983-0-4

Printed in the United States of America

This book is dedicated to "Mama"
Ms. Georgia Lewis
Because the greatest legacy she left me
was a crash course in Grace.

Acknowledgements

First and foremost, I thank God for moving in my life in awesome ways. This book is possible because of the Grace of God; God's Amazing Grace. This book has truly been a labor of love. I thank every person that has ever told me that I needed to write a book. There were many to encourage me, but it was Davita Britton, one of my "Young Ladies," who helped to push me to the cliff. She said one day, in her pushy way, "Te Te, you really need to stop playing around and write this book." Less than a week later Glenn Brown, my brother and friend, kindly pushed me over the cliff. In an unrelated conversation about my car, "the book" came up. He insisted that I could self-publish this book. That same night, (at 11:00pm) he connected me to the person who could provide the assistance to make this book possible and he held my hand with glee during the entire process. Thank you Glenn. Angela Rogers at ADA Unity Publishers was a gift from Glenn and God. Stepping out on faith and a promise, she has truly held my hand, managed my high maintenance, type A personality and still helped me to produce a great book. Her services are in-valuable. William Flowers, what can I say, your cover design is awesome. What a Book Cover! It was the team at *Lifelines* magazine that gave me my picture for this book. I thank Cheryl Mainor for granting me permission for use of the photo and David Jenkins whose photograph graces the cover of this book. A big "Shout Out" to my "title sounding board": Peter, Glenn, Bill, Keith, Angela, Davita, Tyanna, Clinton, Johndalyn and Marguerite. Thanks to my Soror, Ella Vallar, who joined me in a sacrificial fast and prayed with me for 31 days for the success of this book, and to Cathleen Myers who also fasted with me in moral support. No sugar for 31 days was a sacrifice for us all. Lastly, I thank everyone who kept this book in his or her prayers. Thanks for believing God and me. I did it!!!!!!

I give a special Thank You to those who helped to finance the first edition of the printing of this book. I am eternally grateful for your support of my ministry. Thank you, Sorors Deedra Y. Walker, Loretta Martin and Marilyn Barnes; Audrey and Charles Shulruff; Keith Jennings; Reverend, Dr. Jeanne Porter; Reverend Peter Matthews; Reverend Leslie Sanders; Cornell McClellan, Naturally Fit Gym; Scott and Kim Hamilton; and Deidra Cayolle-Amos.

TABLE OF CONTENTS

Foreword

I was diagnosed with HIV/AIDS over seventeen years ago. I believe that I have been infected for at least twenty years. HIV/AIDS came onto the scene twenty-three years ago. This means that I have been infected with HIV for almost the entire pandemic and almost half of my lifetime. In many ways, HIV has defined who I am. I have lived with HIV my entire adult life. How could it not have had a profound impact on me? I never wanted this disease, but I have tried to make the best of a bad situation. Ten years ago, I spoke at my first high school in the city of Chicago, on the topic of HIV/AIDS. Six months later on December 1, 1994, I appeared on the cover of *Essence* magazine in a cover story titled "Facing AIDS." It was a heroic effort for both *Essence* and me. In a climate that was unkind, uncertain and scared of HIV, we rose to the occasion and broke the silence.

I have given a lot of reflection to this journey. Ten years, a decade, is a milestone. Along this journey, I have told my story to magazines, newspapers, news shows, talk shows, and radio shows. I have spoken at countless churches, junior high and high schools and colleges. I believe that I have made up for lost time because the first eight years of my HIV diagnosis, I lived in silence and in secret. By telling my story, I have helped to give HIV/AIDS a face for the African-American Community. God opened the doors and my ministry extended beyond my community. I told my story with the hope and the prayer that those who hear it will never have to feel my pain or walk in my shoes. I have told my story so that others living with adversity will know that they can go on. I have told my story so people will know that there is not one thing in life that should stop them, and nothing that should take their joy. Yes, I even told my story for those who were too ashamed or afraid to tell theirs. I have told my story and will continue to tell, for those who can no longer tell theirs. Especially: *Torey, Wandra, Ronald, Gail, Eric, Deidre, and Dr. Ron.*

I told my story with both confidence and fear. Confidence in knowing that God has ordained me for such a time as this; fear, because you never know how people will respond or even if they will respond. Over the years, people have responded. From the very first day at that very first school...people spoke back to me. This book is a celebration of those who reached out to me. It celebrates those who were touched by my story and those who touched me. I am often reminded, "What comes from the heart, touches the heart." I left myself vulnerable many days, but people, those whose lives I have touched, protected and kept me. I thought it was appropriate that my first book would be a celebration of those who have traveled along this journey with me. Thus, I chronicle my ten years of ministry through their words found in these letters. While these letters chronicle my life and ministry, they also chronicle the life of HIV/AIDS in the past ten years. They reveal the impact that HIV/AIDS has had on individuals, as well as families. These letters reveal the pain caused by HIV. They reflect the discoveries of life HIV forced many to face. They show both the positive and negative attitudes toward HIV. But mostly, these letters reveal the grace, love and faith that people have shown me along my journey.

While these letters speak for themselves, there are many things they do not say. They clearly say, that you prayed for me. I should tell you that God answered your prayers. It is true; the doctors believe that I should have made my transition at least 7-8 years ago. You prayed. My t-cell count has been as low as 8, but as high as 300. You prayed. I have been hospitalized three times, bloody but not bowed. Yes, you prayed.

These letters do not tell you that God has blessed this ministry beyond my human understanding. I have crisscrossed this country speaking to young and old alike. I won an Emmy Award for an on-going series of first-person stories for WBBM-TV Chicago, a CBS affiliate, on my life of living with HIV/AIDS. God has really blessed me. In 2000, I was inducted into Delta Sigma Theta Sorority, Inc., as an honorary member. Wow! In my sorority's 90-year history, we have less than a hundred honorary members. What an honor. I have been blessed. I accepted my call as a minister, proclaiming to preach the Gospel of Jesus Christ. In 2003, I graduated from McCormick Theological Seminary with a Master of Divinity and I am currently working on my PhD in Church History at the Lutheran School of Theology, Chicago. I am truly blessed!

Many of these letters tell you that I found love. But they do not say that I lost love in a course of four years. I am no longer married. I believe that some people are only supposed to be in your life for a season, rather than the entire journey. Although I am no longer married, I am not alone. God fills all the voids. And you know what, as the saying goes and is true for this situation, "one monkey don't stop no show." The fact of the matter, the marriage became unhealthy and I had to make a decision. AIDS had not killed me; he was not going to either, at least not emotionally. So I cut my losses and moved on. Good, bad or indifferent, he certainly has been apart of the journey; therefore, I believe that it is appropriate to add letters that mention my marriage and former husband.

These letters say that I continue to persevere, but they do not say that this disease is an ongoing challenge. While my health is currently stable, life with AIDS is no walk in the park. Contrary to popular belief, (I am told often that I make living with AIDS look easy) I struggle daily. You never see the pain, the guilt and even the shame. I leave these things at the altar. Langston Hughes said it best, "laughing to keep from crying" that is my daily routine. I submit that the best thing that I have going is that I am trying to live and die with dignity and grace; to hold my head up and walk through the shame and pain of this ugly disease.

I am grateful for what these letters say. They speak to the power of the Holy Spirit moving at every phase of my life and ministry. They reveal compassion, pain, joy, hope, faith and love. These letters are a sign of grace; God's Amazing Grace. This grace is the cornerstone of my life, my lifeline. With the grace that God has given me, I was brave enough to tell my story. I opened my heart and people gave me grace. By giving me grace, they found grace for themselves and their families along the way. Travel along my journey of life and ministry through these powerful letters, as they reveal God's Amazing Grace. Please consider this book as the first installment of others to come.

PART ONE

FACING AIDS

REFLECTION: THE ESSENCE ARTICLE

𝒯his article first appeared as a cover story for the December 1994 issue of *Essence* magazine. I am often asked how the cover story came about. Truly, I believe that God's hand was working and weaving in this entire process. In fact, I view the article as a part of and in many ways the launching of an awesome ministry. God used *Essence* magazine and me.

I remember the day I met Susan Taylor, who at the time, was the editor and chief of *Essence*. She and I met at the kick-off banquet for The Expo for Today's Black Woman in Chicago. She was the keynote speaker and I was the recipient of their Community Service Award. I had only been speaking to high school students locally in Chicago for about five months; and the Expo, to my surprise, honored my efforts. The affair was great. Black folks were dressed to kill. And if I might add, I was some kind of sharp, in my Lillie Rubin sequence dress. I was looking so good that men were making advances toward me all night. It did not matter to most men that I had a date or that they had a date. By the time the award was presented, I had been passed at least ten telephone numbers.

I guess people really were not paying attention to what the presenter was saying. Somehow, most people missed the fact that I had HIV and only heard that I was speaking to high school students about HIV/AIDS. When I stood to accept the award, I decided to lay it on the line. After I thanked the Expo for honoring me, I said to the audience, "You know, African-Americans, we are in denial about this disease. Men have been making advances toward me all night. In fact, men with dates have slipped me their telephone numbers. Not only do I have HIV, but I have full-blown AIDS." You could have heard a pin drop. It was as if everyone just stood still at that moment in time. Once I had everyone's attention, I simply said, "We really need to wake-up and begin addressing this disease." I turned to walk off the podium. As I made my way pass Ms. Taylor, she grabbed my arm and asked if *Essence* could do a story on me. I said, "Yes."

Two weeks later, Susan Taylor telephoned and asked if I would grace the cover of her magazine. After I regained my composure, I said, "Ms. Taylor there is not a Black Woman in American who would not want to be on the cover of your magazine. It is an honor. But you do not know anything about me. You only heard me speak for five minutes." She said, "Rae, you have a story to tell and I want to tell it." Truly, the Spirit of God was working and moving in the entire situation. I believe that it was all in divine order. God can work through people who you would least expect and through situations that seem unlikely. That cover story was God's hand working and moving as only God can.

Writing was a painful process. I remember the day I dropped the finished story in the mail. I cried and I cried. It seemed as if I had just given a huge part of myself away. But what I was really doing, in retrospect was creating space for the healing to begin. There is an African Proverb that I quote often which says, "He who conceals his disease cannot expect to be cured." This article was a major step in the healing process.

This article really and truly was a labor of love. After I completed the first draft, *Essence* hired Teresa

Wiltz, a writer from the Chicago area, to revise my version. After a very long interview with Teresa, we had a finished product. I mention this in fairness to Teresa. My story and her creativity gave us the final product. The photo shoot for the cover was twelve hours. Yes, twelve hours for two pictures. In 2000, *Essence* named this article along with two others, one of the most memorable stories in their thirty-year history. Look at God working!

As we approach the tenth anniversary of the December 1994 *Essence* magazine original publication, I thought that it was appropriate to re-publish this article in my first book. It is a significant part of my history and my ministry. Ten years later, I believe that this article still speaks to the current climate around HIV/AIDS in the African-American Community. In many ways, it is more relevant today. African-Americans continue to be disproportionately affected by HIV/AIDS. We are the majority of the AIDS cases in most cities, including those cities where we are the minority in population. Sixty-four percent of all new cases of HIV are African-American Women.

Please, let me introduce to some and present to others, the story that helped to launch my ministry nationally. I hope that my story will help someone today understand that HIV still does not have any boundaries. HIV does not care who you date, how good looking or rich you are, or even what church you attend. It does not care how deep and profound you think your love is. Nor does HIV care how much money you have or about your credentials and education.

If we are going to conquer this disease, African-American Women must move beyond the stereotypes and misconceptions around HIV. We must leave behind this false sense of security and take control of our lives and our bodies. I tell women everyday, "You have no idea what your partner is doing when he is not with you. If he is not in your pocket every second, you do not have a clue." You think you know. Some of us pray that we know, but in the end, you just do not know. This means, in the context of this deadly disease, the only way to be safe is to make a decision to keep yourself safe and free from HIV. It is a great commitment. It is about loving yourself more than you love or want, or think you need a man in your life. When you love yourself more than a man, HIV will not be an issue. At the end of the day, every woman must ask themselves, how much of me am I willing to sacrifice for a man? And every Christian Woman must ask herself, am I really living whole as God intended? Yes, I am still facing AIDS. I also acknowledge that I have been blessed. Who would have thought I would be around for the tenth anniversary of this article? For longevity, I am overjoyed. Yet, I am also sad because the HIV numbers have not decreased, but have risen among Black Women. For those who are reading my story for the first time, I hope that it will help you make a commitment to be safe from HIV/AIDS. In the face of this disease, it is time to re-evaluate our lives. I pray that this article will be catalysis for a commitment to rethink our lives, change some behaviors and turn inward for renewal. For those living with HIV/AIDS, let this article be a reminder that God is able to keep us in the midst of the storm.

Facing AIDS

The day I found out, I was so calm. The counselor noticed it, too. "How am I supposed to be?" I asked her.

"I'm just used to people freaking out on me," she said. "It doesn't mean that you have AIDS. You may never get AIDS. It just means that you are HIV-positive. Do you understand?"

"I'm okay," I told her. I walked out of the American Red Cross office and into the Washington, D.C., sunshine, flagged a cab and went back to work. I worked late that night.

It was 1986 and I was 24. I'd just been given a death sentence.

I am the quintessential Buppie: I'm young - 32. Well educated. Professional. Attractive. Smart. I've been drug- and alcohol-free all my life. I'm a Christian. I've never been promiscuous. Never had an one-night stand. And I am dying of AIDS.

I've been living with the disease for nine years, and people still tell me that I am too pretty and intelligent to have AIDS. But I do. I discovered I was HIV-positive when I tried to give blood at the office. I have no idea who infected me or when it happened.

Still there is one thing I am absolutely certain of: I am dying now because I had one sexual partner too many. And I'm here to tell you one is all it takes.

Make no mistake about it; AIDS is a horrible, sick, foul, filthy disease. I look great to everybody. But I don't feel great. My life is an endless round of doctors' visits, night sweats, chronic yeast infections, debilitating medications and body-numbing fatigue. I've had to give up a promising career as a political

16

organizer. I may never live to finish graduate school. I can't get health insurance. I will never have children. Some days I am filled with rage and despair. Other days I am at peace. I am trying to peacefully coexist with a disease that eats away at my body each and every day. I am its host -- and I don't have any choice in the matter.

I've always been this independent person, the life of the party. My mama locked me out when I was 17, and I've been steppin' ever since. I made a way out of no way. Stayed off the welfare rolls and managed never to get pregnant. I graduated magna cum laude from college. I've worked with and dated the best and the brightest. It's scary that eventually I will have to surrender my independence and my vibrancy to this disease.

But the day I found out my HIV status, I wasn't thinking of dying. I'd already overcome a lot, and I believed there was nothing I couldn't conquer. God never put an obstacle in my way that I couldn't get around. I knew I would be okay.

However, there was one little matter that sent me into a panic: telling the man I was dating. I knew I had to do it. But every time I thought about it, my stomach would twist into knots. We'd used condoms for the entire three or four months we'd been seeing each other, so I was pretty sure he hadn't infected me - nor I him. He was a seminary student studying to be a minister; I was an activist working overtime to help my people. We'd enjoyed some good times-and some good sex. We weren't in love: we were in like.

That night, as I waited for my boyfriend. I did his laundry in the apartment where I lived alone. As I washed and folded his clothes, I tried to still the jitters in my belly.

I told him as soon as he walked in the door, schoolbooks in hand.

"You're what?" he asked.

I took a deep breath and repeated my little bombshell.

"I'm HIV-positive. When I gave blood at the Red Cross they told me I'm HIV-positive."

He chuckled as if he thought I was playing.

"No. I'm very serious," I told him. I immediately gave him the name and number of the place where he should be tested. Just in case.

Then he realized I was serious. "You bitch," he said. As he grabbed his laundry and walked out my door, he declared, "This is over." I never spoke to him again.

That's when the sorrow came. He left, and I was all alone. Damn. I thought. *I'm HIV-positive and the man I was kicking it with just walked out of my life!*

The rest of the night, I called a couple of ex-boyfriends informing them of what had happened and searching for clues as to who had infected me. I cried and cried, and prayed and prayed, and cried some more. The next day, I repeated the process. No man admitted that he had infected me. Not one. No one came to the rescue. Not one. I realized that I was in this alone. There would be no man to take care of me or tell me that it was going to be okay.

Superwoman kicked in. I told myself that this was a small thing – I could overcome anything with the help of God. My childhood had been both dysfunctional and abusive, and very early in my life I believed that God was making me strong. I was sure that I would overcome HIV.

I was referred to the National Institutes of Health (NIH) in Bethesda, Maryland, where I began participating in a long-term study on blood and HIV. With the study I visited a doctor once every six months. There they'd draw my blood for tests and give me a physical exam.

Initially, outside of the study I had no medical treatment for my illness. For years I didn't tell my private physician about my HIV status. I was not sick; there were no symptoms. I pushed AIDS and HIV to the back of my mind. I did minimal reading on the subject. I ignored the television specials. I told only a small group of friends about my con-dition, and the only time we ever discussed it was after my semiannual NIH visit. My buddies were convinced I would never get AIDS. So was I.

In fact, during those first six years, the only two situations where HIV became real for me were during my doctors' visits and when I would meet a man I wanted to date. Then I would have to come clean.

The male problem became easier over time. I found that if a man really wanted to be with me sexually, he would. I didn't yet have AIDS. I looked healthy. Most men-if not all-were willing to go for it. To them HIV seemed to be a small problem easily managed with latex. And I was scrupulous about using condoms; none of the men I dated ever tested positive for HIV.

Meanwhile, the specter of AIDS hovered in the background. Each time I went for my NIH checkup, I anxiously awaited the results. Had the virus progressed to AIDS? I would get my answer in writing, and each time the result was the same: My immune system was stable. The virus was not active. I found great comfort in this bit of news. It helped me to continue my life the same way I had before.

After four years I began taking AZT, a drug prescribed for HIV patients to delay the progression of the virus. I was told the medication was not a big deal; the side effects would be minimal and would last no longer than about three weeks. If only I had been so lucky: My body rejected the medicine for almost six months. I was constantly nauseated and had excruciating headaches that lasted for days, even weeks at a time. I gained 15 pounds and sneaked naps every available second. Still, I suffered in secret, finishing my undergraduate degree and senior honors thesis while working part-time. Superwoman returned. The AZT would keep AIDS at bay.

But it wasn't to last. By winter 1992, the worst was confirmed: I had AIDS. I really had AIDS. I sank into a deep depression.

So far I haven't been hospitalized. But there have been problems. When I visited Paris last year, my period started a week early. It continued for 22 days. Another time my period lasted for an hour. My doctor said, "It's dysfunctional uterine bleeding. Women with AIDS get that all the time." I'm getting used to the irregularities.

What's harder to get used to is the side effects of the nine to 14 pills that I swallow each day. One drug, ddI (an antiretroviral medication), gave me extreme diarrhea. It was horrible. I had no control.

Not so long ago, my doctor noticed that I'd lost weight. I didn't think much of it until the day I went shopping for a New Year's Eve dress. I grabbed a bunch of size 10's. I tried them all on. Then I went back and got some 8's. I eventually bought a size 4. Me, who'd always fluctuated between a 10 and a 12. I mean, I was built like a sistah! I had *meat* on my bones. But no more. That day I cried.

Through it all, my friends have been very supportive, very pushy. Because I'm not on the best of terms with either my birth mother or the woman who raised me, my friends are my family. One friend is always bugging me to come over for dinner. Another will drive across town to tempt me with food. They put a lot of pressure on me. "If you think healthy," they say, "you'll be healthy."

It's easy for them to say that because I still look well; but my friends don't see me when I'm in too much pain to get out of bed. They don't see the illness. And I feel like screaming, "Don't you get it? I'm not going to be okay. I have AIDS!"

But somewhere in the midst of my grief, I slowly began to gain some control. I started seeing a therapist twice a week. Antidepressants reined in my emotions. I read everything I could find on AIDS and HIV.

Yet I was lonely, so lonely. I dreaded coming home to an empty house, with no one waiting for me. But home was my only refuge-the one place where I could hide from this ugly disease.

Dating meant rejection and false hope, though men were still attracted to me. When I met men, I didn't waste a lot of time. After several dates, I told them of my illness. Some were brave enough to spend time with me. But invariably, after several weeks or months, it would prove too much. They couldn't handle the magnitude of the illness: the depression, the pills, the diarrhea, the despair, and ultimately the fear of infection. One brother, a successful businessman, often called just to see if I still had AIDS. Eventually I told him to stop calling. It was just too painful.

I felt isolated. Damaged. My anger at God was profound, and I questioned Him often. What were the lessons in dying? Was He punishing me? Forsaking me? Hadn't I suffered enough as a child? I tried to live my life by the example that Christ set. What had I done wrong?

Superwoman was exhausted. Living with AIDS was too complex. Yes, I was tired, but my spirit wanted to go on. I understood that the person I used to be was gone. The new person had AIDS. Could there be a way to live in peace with my disease? I went within myself for the answers. I surrendered to God. I just let go.

It was then that I found answers. The first step in the healing process was to move beyond the shame and stigma of having AIDS. For six years I had hidden my secret from all but a handful of my closest friends. When I came out with my illness, it felt as if tons of bricks had been lifted off my body. I told people at work. I told all my friends. Gossip moved quickly, but the response was overwhelming. People reached out to me in a special way. My support base became strong and powerful. Last March I told the woman who raised me that I was sick. Telling Mama was the hardest thing I've had to do. She still won't accept that I'm dying. She tells me the doctors must be wrong. And I tell her again and again, "Mom, it's been nine years. I know."

I buried Superwoman. And in doing so I found my strengths. One day I was asked to speak to some high-school students about my disease. The prospect frightened me. But as I stood in front of those kids, with nothing prepared and with no idea of where to begin, I asked God to simply use me. The words poured out. Some students cried. Others missed class to hear me speak again. One such student worked her way into my life. We talk often. I try to keep her out of trouble and on the right track.

More than a year and perhaps 70,000 high school students later, I understand that my suffering is not in vain. I just have to tell the story-as a lesson for others. I talk to young people not just about AIDS but also about destructive sexual behavior, about taking control of their bodies before it is too late.

Surrendering myself to God is the smartest decision I have made in this odyssey. As I let go of the old person, God created a new one. This new Rae has a purpose. What I discovered was that God uses us in ways not of our own understanding. And once you let go and let God, He reveals the plan. When you accept it, blessings flow.

And my blessings are abundant. I have not worked in more than a year, but I've never done without. I recently married. Only when I defined my new life with AIDS did I open my mind and heart to a nice guy. And that's just what I got--a nice guy. I met Kenny through my minister early this year and knew right away he was my soul mate. God sent me a man grounded in Christianity and bursting with compassion, love-and fun.

Nonetheless, the disease continues to progress in my body. Managing AIDS is a full-time job. My immune system is impaired. At last count my T-cells were at an all-time low of 66. I often have night sweats. I spend days at a time in bed. Where it once was hidden, AIDS has now become a very real part of my life.

What I have clearly learned is that, unlike people, AIDS does not discriminate. My wish is that all women would realize this and take control of their lives and their bodies. To not use a condom in this day and age is *suicide*.

I can see the light at the end of the tunnel. Of course there are some bad times. I am sad some days. Other days I am scared, and I'm terrified of the destruction AIDS is causing to my body. Some nights I cry long and hard. The difference now is that I have someone to hold me and wipe the tears. And most important, I don't wallow in the sadness. Kenny wipes the tears, and I keep going.

The misery, the despair, the hopelessness are gone. Of course I am dying. But I will live until I do!

*Rae Lewis-Thornton told her story to Teresa Wiltz, a fashion writer with the **Chicago Tribune**.*

* * *

REFLECTION: ESSENCE LETTERS

I was really naïve about the impact of the *Essence* article in the very beginning. I had no idea how ground breaking the article would be. As I reflect, it took a lot of courage and a lot of guts. There were many reactions. People talked and talked about that article. It was the most amazing thing for me to stand in the line at the grocery store and listen to people talk about me as they glanced through the article at the check out counter. At times it was painful, but mostly a little funny. At first, I was not recognized because I cut my hair really short right after the photo shoot. Also, because of HIV, I was still losing weight. Many times, people had no idea that they were talking about me. The typical conversation was that the girl on the cover of *Essence* was a model, but she was a different woman from the one on the inside who has AIDS. People would actually debate it. Sometimes, I would intervene, but mostly, I let them resolve it themselves.

In retrospect, that cover story was the making of history. In that process, I was clueless. The impact of the article has been illustrated on its own terms. Over the years, it has continually been referred to as the story that gave AIDS a face for the African-American Community. Equally important, through my willingness to be vulnerable, I gave African-American Women a face for AIDS that they could relate to. By doing so, I brought this deadly disease a lot closer to home. For this, I am particularly proud.

This issue of *Essence* still remains one of their most popular. African-Americans of all ages read my story. Over the years, people have expressed to me the impact that the article has had on their lives. I have

25

heard many stories. Like the woman who approached me three years ago in the hair salon to tell me that, "I help save her life." Of course, when one is approached with such news, there are many first reactions of which none you reveal to the person who has approached you. Silence was always my best policy until they finished their story. This particular woman told me that she read my *Essence* article and made a decision to become celibate. She was a little scared and decided in the face of HIV/AIDS to take some time and re-evaluate her dating and sex life. The man that she had just begun dating decided that he could no longer date her on her terms. She said, "I walked away. That was the best thing I could have done. His family buried him last year. He died from AIDS." My stomach dropped and my heart sank with both joy and pain. One lost and one saved from this deadly disease. In many ways, this was a common reaction from African-American Women. They often tell me that my story forced them to re-evaluate their dating and sex life. My hope is that such a re-evaluation would keep them safe and free from HIV, so they would never have to feel my pain up close and personal.

One of the cutest stories came from a guy who ran the post office in his small rural town. He told me that two African-American Pre-teens picked up their parents mail, which included the *Essence* magazine. They started talking about how "fine" I was. Then one of the young guys said, "Man, she has AIDS." They started a debate that led them to the pages of the article. The postmaster said that "they stood in the middle of the floor and read the entire story," he added, "Any article that would command the attention of young African-

American Men deserves to be posted, that is why your article is hanging on the wall of my post office."

People are amazing. This article taught me that when you truly leave yourself open and vulnerable, people would not disappoint you. The saying, "What comes from the heart touches the heart" is the best way to covey the response to the *Essence* article from the African-American Community. You know, women mostly, still bring me their copy of the magazine to autograph as I travel the country. Sometimes, the magazine is in mint condition, almost ten years later. Wow! My copy has no eyes. Just the other day in Hallmark, a woman told me that her copy of the article has been with her to three states.

In the months following the publication of the article, I received hundreds of letters. (Of which I still have.) There were many different expressions. Some wanted me to know that I opened their eyes. Some wanted me to know that there were other women like me living with HIV/AIDS, but not free to disclose. Some thanked me for my courage and some prayed for me. In all of them, there was a touch of grace; Amazing Grace. These are just some of the letters I received in response to the *Essence* article.

Dear Rae,

Hello my name is Khamishah. I'm not sure if your remember me or not. I'm a senior at Hyde Park Career Academy. On the first day you came to our school, I showed you around. I was Mr. Slater's helper. Just in case you don't remember I've enclosed a picture of me. (Go ahead! Look! I'll wait!). Welcome back! I hope you remember me. Recently, I saw you on the front cover of Essence magazine. I just want to say that you look fantastic, you and your husband look so blessed. I am a young warrior for Christ. It really makes me happy to see the Lord working through you both. You have changed a lot of lives since you spoke at my school. The Lord brings all of his family together to teach, to help, to share, and to LOVE. You both have done exactly that. You have filled my life with so much joy. As you talked, your words went straight to my heart. I cannot say that I understand what you're going through because I don't. I do, however, love to be a young warrior for Christ. There is so much in the world that Satan will try to throw at you, but I know I will make it through and so will you. May GOD continue to bless and keep you and Mr. Thornton. I'm sure I speak for all of Hyde Park when I say we would love for you to come back and visit us again.

Khamishah

This letter really touched me because it came from a student from one of the first five schools where I spoke about HIV/AIDS. This young lady taking the time to write, only confirmed the special relationship established with this group of young people. I made so many friends at Hyde Park Career Academy. The school has continually supported my work on HIV over the years. This was truly one group of young people that was transformed by my presence and ministry. In fact, overall, my first few months speaking to students in Chicago public high schools remain special and dear to my heart. I often joke that I am so popular with these young people that I could probably run for office in Chicago and win. Remember, they are now voting age.

Just A Little Something
By Khamishah

Sometimes we go through something that seems so tough, and even though the road seems smooth it's often kind of rough.

It's such a hard struggle and you're too tired to fight, even though you've conquered one day you're sure tomorrow won't be so bright.

I thought you should know no matter what you do, there's a silent prayer going straight to God for you.

It's there when you need it or even if you don't, it moves all the time even if you won't.

So you're not alone no matter what, this prayer will never go. This is just a little something I thought that you should know.

Dear Rae,

Sister, I just read your article in Essence. As a 29-year-old black professional female I can relate to your world. Your added obstacle of AIDS provides a tough journey I'm sure. I am so glad to hear that you surrendered to God- your strength, faith, and belief will carry you as well as the love and prayers from around the globe. Even though I only know you from this article - God has selected you for a reason beyond our understanding. You are truly an angel- in appearance, wisdom, and experience. I wish you peace, divine order, love - your spirit has made a big difference in my heart. Thank you for your message, thank you for caring, thank you for being born, thank you for being a living angel. Know that God surrounds you.

Peace & Joy,
Bronwyn

To Whom It May Concern:

I really would like to thank Rae Lewis-Thornton on her being so open about the AIDS disease that has stricken her. I read the article and I was deeply touched. I laid the magazine down in a way that my boyfriend would see it. At first he noticed the pretty lady on the cover and then he saw that she has AIDS, he began reading. I saw him in a way that I had never seen before. I saw the concern and the worriedness on his face and in his eyes. We knew about AIDS but we thought that people with full-blown AIDS would some how show it. I mean we thought that she would have had scares or spots and even look frail or sickly. That goes to show that everything that looks good ain't always good. She has really opened our eyes. Again thank you Rae Lewis-Thornton on your courage and openness.

Stay strong and may God be with you and everyone else that has to face this awful disease.

Sincerely,
Verna

Dear Mrs. Thornton,

Hi, my name is Rondesha and I attend Palm Beach Comm. College. I read your story in Essence and I want you to know that it changed my life. I am not sexually active; I am a Christian but those desires come I just never fall into the devil's trap. When I read your story it gave me another look at my life and my body as a temple for the Holy Spirit. It must stay pure until I get married. I wish right now I could give my life so that you can continue your life because you have a lot to offer. You are a black, very educated young woman and a role model something we don't have a lot of. I read it, it touch my life in another way. I want you to know <u>Jesus never fails</u> so don't you give up.

Thanks you,
Rondesha

When one embarks on a ministry such as mine, you live for such a letter. Rondesha is only a reflection of the many other young women who expressed the same sentiments after reading the *Essence* article.

Rae,

My sister, my beautiful, beautiful sister. Every time I receive Essence, I look and exclaim over how pretty the model looks. When I saw you I did the same until I read the caption next to your solemn face. Then I gasped and thought "My God" I cannot relate to how much your confession touches me. My heart feels so sad, so heavy. I cried. I cry as I write this to you. Maybe it's because we're both black women possibly because we are both young educated (I'm still in college) and drug-free but most overwhelmingly it's because we are both human. Blood, warm blood runs through my veins too. I have experienced pain and I have only begun to experience life at 20 yrs. old. The same for you in a since. You may be wondering why I'm writing you and in an odd way I really don't know. I just felt an immediate need to tell you the kind of response I had as a result of reading your article. And even though we have never met and may never will, I love you. I do with all my heart and soul. Because whenever something happens to someone of my ethnicity I feel towards it. If they commit a hideous crime I cringe and wonder about their background and circumstances, which led to it and it probably could have been prevented. If they receive high honors or praise by the media my heart smiles.

So when I say that I truly love you, it is not because I feel sorry for you it is because...well honestly it is partly that. But it is mainly because I relate to you. You are my sister. If you aren't *feeling too tired, I would appreciate very much to hear from you by letter or phone. I'll pray for you but I have been for so long before I couldn't put a name to your unfamiliar face because every day I ask God to help and watch over my people. But now I will personally ask for you.*

May God Bless You!
(smile)
Love Erika

P.S. Before I received this issue I was feeling down due to very selfish reasons. Now, I see that may be I should look outside of myself a little more to see that the world is bigger than just me.

Rae Lewis-Thornton

Thanks so much for sharing your story with me. "Facing Aids" December 1994. I love you for your courage, your spunk and your "never give up" attitude. You know living according to GOD's will is a difficult task for many of us. Thanks for making it look so easy. I look forward to hearing from you again, because I know you're going to be around a while. (GOD has plans for you.) Keep on Fighting!

Jeneise

Dear Sister,

I hope you are in good spirit when this letter and card reaches you. If not, I hope it does just that. I am writing to express my love for you and to let your know I care. Your story of HIV and AIDS touched my heart and soul. I was moved to send you some kind of a note. Like you, I began to ask why? But my faith Islam teaches unexpected. Which I usually find difficult to do because I am a very emotional person. My sister and I are trying to respect the will of Allah to be done in my life also. I pray that Allah will let you teach me another way. This letter is about love for another human being to let you know you are in my heart and prayers. May the almighty Allah continue to bless you and your husband everyday of your life. Stay strong my sister and brother in your faith (God Bless).

Assalaam Alaikium,
Lukmon

To Whom It May Concern:

I must say, I was truly touched by the article about the sister with AIDS. It made me re-evaluate my past sexual relationships and myself. I've been abstinence for a couple of months now. The thought of actually going to get tested for AIDS scares me to death, but I know in my heart it's the right and responsible thing to do. I am also young, educated, and drug free.

Sincerely yours,
So much in common

Thank you for printing "Facing AIDS" by Rae Lewis-Thornton. It really hit close to home because I too contracted a disease at a young age. I was turning 18 when I was told I had Herpes. The guy didn't want to admit he gave it to me. I went through feelings of denial, anger and finally acceptance. It's hard to tell guys, but I come as a package disease and all. I found someone to love me as that package. Women save yourself for someone deserving.

R.C.

Dear Rae,

I was touched by your compassionate and courageous story, written in the December issue of *Essence*. You have since been in my prayers and in my thoughts. The article was so compelling; I felt every emotion you described. What makes your battle so empathetic is God's obvious presence in your life. In the midst of all you've endured, God has brought you...a mighty ways.

I thank God for all of His goodness and mercy. He is worthy to be praised for not only allowing you the opportunity to minister to our younger brothers and sisters, but to adults as well. From one African American sister to another, I honestly wish I could say or do something to ease your pain. As Christians we often ask. "Why Us," the truth is, "Why Not Us." If we are born to do His will, why not go all the way! (Just as our savior). I was glad to read that you have found inner peace. Most of us live our whole lives... searching!

Two years ago, I remember visiting my girlfriend Rita in Baltimore and she asking, if I mind visiting her friend Henry, who has AIDS. Rita said she would understand if I was uncomfortable but that it was important that she see him. Having never been around anyone who was really sick or one who has AIDS, I told Rita, no. It was just too much to handle even for a Christian! Embarrassed by my own reaction and feelings, I reluctantly changed my mind.

I prayed in silent all the way to his house. I kept wondering, if my God has never failed me, why was I having so much trouble. We arrived at the house he lives in an apartment on the third floor. As I began to walk up the stairs, I started to shake. His apartment seemed so far from the front door. Finally, when Rita tapped on the door, I took a deep breath and dried my sweaty palms. Well lo and behold...we were greeted by a warm and adorable man. My anxiety went right out of his kitchen bay window. I was impressed. Henry's taste is impeccable. He has many talents, one of which is the gift to gab. In a short time, I felt as if I had known him for years. We laughed, drank tea and had a good ole time. After about an hour, Rita said that we had to be going. I was truly disappointed, another 10 minutes; I would have probably taken off my shoes. I gave Henry a big hug and told him that I wanted to see him again. That was probably one of the best weekends I have ever had.

The following Sunday, when I was back home in New York and sitting in worship service, it dawned on me...that I had a testimony!

Everyone was touched by my story of meeting Henry. I told the group that I wanted something special for him. We sent him a nice care package along with some Christian reading material...Rita later told me ...he loved it!

My last report was that he takes each day as it comes...but basically he is doing all right. I thank God for the way he's turned my anxiety and fear into love.

Rae, I wish you and your family the very best. Spiritually, I feel we've already met, so if our path don't cross here on earth, I look forward to meeting you on the other side, along with all of our other courageous and memorable brothers and sisters.

Elexis

Dear Rae,

Finally, someone at Essence realized that there was an issue more important than how to catch a man or enlightens Black Women on why all the good men are gay.

When I walked into my mother's house for Thanksgiving dinner and saw the December 1994 issue of Essence, I was truly touched that someone felt that an issue such as AIDS should be a cover story. As we all know, AIDS is a life threatening disease to all living beings. However, it must be emphasized that AIDS is and will continue to impair black-life.

The timing for this issue is perfect, since the holidays are a time to reflect and remember our hopes. I like to reflect on the true essence of a black woman, not how she looks; but how she embraces good and bad experiences. And my hope is that this disease will come to an end soon for everyone sake!

Merry Christmas Rae!

Dear Rae,

I have wanted to write this letter ever since your article in the Essence magazine 1994. I have always wanted to say you changed my life in a way and you made me take that step in getting an AIDS test. Seeing you on the front of the magazine made me think a lot. I had thought about taking it before but always found a reason not to do it - but you changed my mind-reading the article on how you had to accept that your outlook on life would have too change and your fears and feelings. I thought you were really brave to share your illness with others especially the Black Community - we have a knack for closing our eyes to heath issues especially to this illness. I propose we feel that only white people and gay can get the illness, but it is like someone said illness isn't prejudice it has no class and that this illness is now entering people of straight (men and women) relationships. When I see people just go from man to man - woman to woman and think that this illness will not affect them-if they don't think about it, it will happen to them. Basically I wish to thank you. I had one and I thank God it was negative. I also got a friend of mine to get one - after I told her about you and she was also negative. You described the pain you go through, and praying helps and I was pleased to hear that you found a black man who loved you for you, and even married. I wish both of you love, happiness, and faith. Never let go of hope, faith and always remember when we think we are alone in our pain and you want it and we are never alone, because God is always there and always remember He loves us. I have an illness; it's called Panic and Anxiety Disorder, which controlled my life in many ways - bodily, emotionally, mentally and physically. When I had bad attacks, I would be completely washed out because it drains you out of every little bit of energy. Every muscle and nerve in your body goes mad. But I am now learning to cope with it. The attacks are less or more controllable now and changing my thinking, diet, but mainly me. It has had an advantage it has brought my mother and me closer in so many ways. Anyway I wish you health and goodness in life and that you keep that courage, and never give up hope I want to say more but I will stop with God Bless you. You are in my thoughts.

Angella

Dear Mrs. Thornton,

I'm writing to let you know how your article turned my life around; and lead me back to Christ.

I admire you, I love you sister. Your strength has given me a new hope in Jesus; I was feeling real low the day I read you story, I thought here's another depressing story, but instead it uplifted me and let me know that through adversity God will prevail.

Love, Phoebe

41

Dear Rae,

I'm writing to personally "thank you" for your courage and strength to offer your story to all of us! When I read the article and you described yourself, I thought of my friends as well as myself. Since I had read the article, I've talked to my male friend about the article as well as my brother.

My brother gets tested every year on his job. He's negative and so is his girlfriend who I call "Happy Go Lucky!" She's so sweet.

My male friend says he has been tested twice. Once when he was hired for his new job (14 months ago) and then again six months later. I haven't seen the test results myself. I asked him to go with me to get tested so that I can be comfortable about both of us and the relationship. It had got hot and heavy on the couch but no intercourse. I've been tested in December '94. My results were negative. My male friend still has not gone to the clinic to be tested. So I say, "No blood, no results (papers), no groove, no love!"

I do respect my body. I'm writing to tell you that I plan to honor your wish "that we take control of our bodies and our lives."

I found this card in an African bookstore and thought of you. Rae, please know that all your sisters (especially your "sistahs") pray for you. I know I do. God's arms are around you keep the faith.

Joycelyn

Dear Mrs. Thornton,

Mrs. Thornton, I have just finished reading your magazine article. I don't know what to say. I can't believe that a woman so beautiful, so intelligent, and so young can be dying. You know Mrs. Thornton, I sometimes wonder why such a disease exists and why our sophisticated technology, hasn't found a cure. Mrs. Thornton, I truly believe that God is the only cure for this dreadful disease! He says to you and I that "if you have the faith of a mustered seed, you can move mountains." Mrs. Thornton, keep the faith and the Lord will move this mountain out of your life.

Mrs. Thornton, don't ever feel like you are by yourself. God is always with you. He is there when you think no one is there! He knows what you're going through when you think no one knows! Just put all your troubles, heartaches, and worries in his hands and everything will be all right.

In conclusion, let me say that sometimes we forget who God is and what he is capable of. God is omnipotent an omniscient. In my church, we sometimes sing *Jesus Will Work It Out*. If you let... Let Jesus work it out!

Your friend,
Donald

Dear Ms. Lewis-Thornton:

You are beautiful and brave! Thank you from the bottom of my heart, for sharing your "Facing AIDS" story in the December 1994 issue of Essence magazine. Your article moved me to tears because I realized that "Facing AIDS" could have been about me. I am also a young, well-educated, drug-free, attractive, smart, professional, non-promiscuous, African-American, Christian Woman.

I was shocked to learn that AIDS is now the third leading cause of death for women of color between ages 15 and 44. The fact that seventy-four percent of women with AIDS are African-American or Latina floored me. And, I was horrified to read that seventy-three of 100,000 African-American Women have AIDS.

I was so touched by your courage and tenderness in telling your story that I hosted a rap session about AIDS several weeks ago in my home.

About a dozen of my girl friends between ages 15 and 40 came, including an Infection Control Nurse who was our guest speaker. We talked and answered questions about AIDS for more than two hours.

Your "Facing AIDS" story was the beginning of our discussion, and they too were touched by your beauty and bravery. Safe sex, abstinence, and HIV screening/education were among the topics we discussed. And in our hearts, we all vowed to tell at least one other person about AIDS.

We had conversation in a way that we had never talked before and it was all because of you and your precious article. As a matter of fact, the 15-year-old who attended, bless her heart, asked when we would meet again so she could bring high school friends along.

I wholeheartedly believe that thousand of lives were touched by your story, and perhaps thousands will be saved. Thank you and God bless you.

Sincerely,
Stacy

Hi Rae Lewis-Thornton,

When I first glanced at December Essence, I couldn't believe it you look so healthy. Then when I proceeded to read your article, I couldn't put it down without writing you this letter of Thanks. I thank you for writing your story in Essence, for African Women everywhere needed to hear your message that getting AIDS can happen to us and me included if we don't practice safe sex. Also in closing, I'm glad to see you believe in God. Stand strong in your faith for He will see you through.

God Bless you and yours,
Geraldine

Rae,

How fitting that your name brings to mind a word associated with light:

Ray (ra) n 1. a thin line narrow beam or radiation, esp. one of visible light, one of the lines of light that appear to radiate from a bright object 2. a small amount; trace; a ray of hope.

You courageously brought to light a subject that unfortunately a lot of us try to keep in the dark. Without a doubt you give hope that there can be life in the face of death and for this I say thank you. Your story will forever live in my heart and mind and although physically none of us will remain on this earth eternally (thank goodness!!) I know you will continue to live, you'll just be moving to an address where other angels such as yourself dwell.

I love you my sister,
Celesto

P.S. I know you're probably busy, but if at all possible please contact me. I have some personal concerns about HIV and AIDS and I have no one to talk to. I'm only 25 years old but the few times I've engaged in sexual intercourse it was mostly unprotected I pray that if someday I share your fate that I will be as strong but I must admit that in the meantime I spend a lot of time afraid (nightmares etc.) After reading your article I've made a promise of celibacy to myself not just because of all other risk but because it's a sin. I've been committing for way to long. I hope to hear from you soon.

* * *

MRS. YOUNGBLOOD'S CLASS

It is not uncommon for me today to get letters from classes and study groups who use the *Essence* article as an educational tool. In fact, over the years, I have given permission for the article to be reprinted in the National Red Cross training manual on HIV/AIDS and even some college level books, such as the Freshman Orientation book at Hampton University. Most recently, I granted reprinting permission for a book that will primarily be used in college level literature classes. However, in the first months of the *Essence* article, I was taken by complete surprise when I received these letters from Mrs. Youngblood's 5th grade class.

First, I was surprised that a teacher would think to utilize this article in such a creative way. Secondly, the response of the children was overwhelming. They were simple, yet at the same time they were profound. Some felt genuinely sorry and concerned, which for me illustrates the humanity of young people. Think about the context in which this article was published and these particular letters written. AIDS was still very much a taboo disease. In fact, at this time, Ryan White the young boy from Indiana, who had so much courage, infected with HIV from blood products because he was hemophilia, was being discriminated against. He was actually kicked-out of school.

These letters suggest, at least to me, that when young people are given all the information on their terms and on their level, they will in the end decide for themselves. They do not wakeup hating or discriminating. They are taught these things. These letters also illustrate the impact HIV/AIDS can have on the lives of young people and it clearly illustrates that no single family is exempt from this disease. But mostly, these letters show how young people reached out to me and extended just a little more grace. When I received these letters, I was so touched. At the same time, I wanted to reach out to them. My story had touched their lives, but I wanted it to be more than an educational exercise. I wanted them to never have to walk my path or feel my pain. Yet I know that they, in the end, would have to make their own choices and live their own lives.

Ten years later, my continued prayer is that these young people kept themselves safe and free from the destructive path of HIV/AIDS. They are young adults now, between the ages of 19-21. Even to this day, I pray that they remember my story and use it as a stepping-stone to make responsible and healthy choices. I hope that they remember. Meet Mrs. Youngblood's 5th grade class.

Dear Ms. Thornton,

I understand how you feel about AIDS. My step uncle has AIDS and I am very very sad. He was in the hospital for a longtime and I really missed him. I missed him because he was very nice. I also missed him because he worked at Toby's and he gave me and my brother free ice pops. He is still alive and he just went out of town. If I lost my uncle, I would visit his grave everyday. He is not that old. He is around forty.

I wish that there were a cure for AIDS. I would pay $50,000 to the person that could find the cure. I would give free learning for people who wanted to work on AIDS research.

I would stop people from having sex without a condom. And I would solve the drug problem.

Thank you for sharing your article with me. Please write back.

Your friend,
Mary

Dear Mrs. Lewis-Thornton,

Hello. My name is Shawntrice. I'm in Mrs. Youngblood's 5th grade class. I read your article and I understand some of the things you're going through. Keep surrendering yourself to God. Put yourself in His hands. I'm a Christian and so I'll pray really hard for you just as I pray for my Uncle Willie, Great Grandmother, and my lovely Aunt Tonya.

If I had a powerful role such as president, I would probably stop AIDS by praying. I would try to do anything to help you. Hang in there. You'll make it through.

Sincerely yours,
Shawntrice

Dear Rae,

I understand the problem you are going through. AIDS is a very serious disease that you can't get rid of.

My cousin was a victim of AIDS. He got it through unprotected sex. He died leaving the family with sorrow. Our love for him still last. We buried him where he was born.

You can get AIDS by unprotected sex, dirty needles. I'm going to protect myself by saying no to sex till I'm properly married. I will never use dirty needles and I will never use drugs.

Sincerely,
Monica

Dear Rae Thornton,

I think you should share your story all over the world. The reason you should share your story all over the world is because people need to be educated. I think you are very pretty. And I'm sorry this had to happen to you. If I had AIDS, I wouldn't be able to handle the pain. I'm glad that you finally found someone to love you for you because everyone in this world needs to feel loved. I'm also glad that I got the chance to read your story because it helped me realize that it could happen to anyone. You're in my prayers.

Sincerely,
Ambiance

Dear Rae,

I know how it feels to live with this disease that eats your body away everyday. This disease is a killer. The man you got married to, I think he is a very intelligent gentleman. Because he stands by your side everyday.

I think you are very pretty and I hope the person that infected you comes forward. My name is Caniesha and I hope you continue to educate, high school, elementary, and middle school students.

Sincerely,
Caniesha

* * *

PART TWO

WHEN I SPEAK

REFLECTION: WHEN I SPEAK

$\mathcal{I}$n the past ten years, I have crisscrossed this country speaking about the impact HIV/AIDS has had on my life. I have never turned down a speaking request unless there was a conflict in scheduling or I was too sick to stand on my feet. I mean that literally, because I have spoken many times sick. I have spoken with a fever of a 105, fatigue, diarrhea, nerve pain and even pneumonia. I have made it to speaking engagements so nauseated from the medication that the school officials had to track down crackers in the school cafeteria to calm my stomach before I spoke. Recently, while at Spelman College, I had diarrhea so bad that I almost did not make it to the bathroom. It does not matter my condition; still I rise. Strangely enough, I find that God does God's best work when I am sick. Typically, those times have been my most impactful speaking engagements. The Apostle Paul ex-presses it best: "My strength is made perfect in weak-ness." (2 Cor 12:9 KJV)

Traveling and speaking is a hard life. People think it is glamorous, but it is not. Airports, hotels, and always having to be "on" is a lot of work. People never really let you rest. There are very few private moments. Being in the public arena all the time can also be a lonely place. It is never about you, but about what you do for others. I even discovered that everyone does not have your best interest at heart. I have road stories for you, like when I stayed at the hotel, which was the local spot for prostitutes to conduct business. Honestly, sometimes I get weary, even discouraged. But in the end, this is an emotion that I cannot afford to hold on to. I am always reminded of an old saying "to whom much is given, much is required." I accept the challenges of being a public speaker and "keep on truckin' baby."

I do believe that God has given me an awesome ministry. I believe that God has placed me here for such a time as this. To be able to affect lives is an incredible responsibility. Sometimes, it is a heavy one. I have to stay "prayed up," so that I am clear that God is the moving force and Rae is not interfering in the game. People invite me to speak mostly on the topic of HIV/ AIDS. Over the years, I have discovered that AIDS is the catalyst that gets me through the door. How God uses me once I am there, unfolds each time I speak. I am some-times amazed at the miracles that take place at my speaking engagements.

My message is much broader than HIV/AIDS. God weaves my whole life experience into every speech. My audiences have "aha moments" all the time. Sometimes it is about AIDS, other times it is about surviving childhood sexual abuse or it is simply about hanging in and not giving up. Believe it or not, I have never written a speech. Nor am I ever quite sure what will be said or how people will respond. For sure, my presentations are live and unrehearsed. This has offended some people's sensibilities. Over the years, I have become milder, more introspective; I think. I do not "cuss," (thank the Lord) as much. But my boldness and candor has not altered, nor will it ever. I think my candor is scary for some. But the alternative is even scarier and I believe it is even more offensive to stand before people with half-truths. Plus, AIDS is ugly; why should I make it pretty or more palpable. You may miss the point.

I am certain that each time I speak, God moves. God uses my life to help others. I heard my Pastor say, "There is glory in my story." Someone's life; their joy; their deliverance; their "aha" moments are connected to me telling my story. If I am not where I am suppose to be, doing what I do, they cannot get where God wants them to be. It is simple; my testimony will help to move people in the right direction of their testimony.

However, I must admit that the human in me gets tried. When I see the statistics of 40,000 new cases of HIV yearly in the United States, with most of them African-American Women, I falter for a moment and wonder if I am really making an impact. For sure, I have been disheartened; like the time, I met the nineteen year old, pregnant young woman in the HIV Clinic who heard me speak when she was a freshman in high school and still became HIV infected. I remember that day she told me, "I heard you speak when I was a freshman in high school." She added, "And I thought that you were a good speaker." It felt like she had stuck a knife into my heart. I do not speak because I want people to think I am a good speaker. I speak so those who hear my story will never have to walk in my shoes. I know in the end that every person has to choose his or her own path, but a story like this one does hurt the spirit. Although there are some disappointments, there are also some victories.

At the end of each day, I ask, am I really making a difference? Then the mail comes, one letter at a time. The letters in this section are a reflection of the hundreds that have been sent my way after a speaking engagement. These letters reveal the victories. They reveal the "miracle working stuff" in my ministry. I thank God for the miracle in each letter, for the grace that flows with the "stroke of the pen."

Dear Ms. Thornton,

Thank you very much for coming to my school, King Lab, to talk to us about AIDS, yourself, and life.

I and many other people (my friends, teachers, etc.) truly appreciated your talk. It came through to us much stronger than all the others we have heard. Most speakers talk to us in a way that we feel lower than them. You talked to us as your equal. Another thing that most speakers do is talk only about AIDS and how you can get it. After we hear the same thing over and over again it can get boring. Sure, you skinned these topics but then you talked about your life and how important life is. Also, you spoke completely at our level. This was a wonderful thing for us kids.

You touched everyone so much that after your talk while I was in class the teacher (you might know her, Ms. Levy) was so moved that she couldn't teach us! (We were having a special rehearsal for the MLK Assembly.

Thank you,
Emiko

Dear Ms. Thornton,

My name is Jordann. I am an eighth grade student at the University of Chicago Laboratory School where you recently spoke. I am writing this letter to tell you how much your words meant to me and how deeply you moved me.

After you spoke to my class, I really began to think about life and the choices I make. You see, I really realized there are real, even life's threatening consequences in every choice you make. As I walked out of the auditorium after hearing the most important message I think I'll ever hear in my life, I decided that when I grow up, I should be fortunate enough to have the strength and courage that I saw in you. I believe that you were sent to us, to deliver a message that is, and will continue to affect me as long as I live. I really think you are a hero, and you are my role model. I hope that someday, I can affect some bodies' life, as much as you have affected mine.

Thank you!
Sincerely,
Jordann

Hi Rae,

Hi! How are you doing? I'm doing okay. If you don't know who I am, I am the one and only white girl at the teen conference in Columbus. I feel you made a big impact on my life. From here on out I'm going to be picky who I choose to sleep with. Also I know more about AIDS then before I stepped in the door. I've always told my family I would stop sleeping around and never kept my word but I think since I've met someone AIDS infected. All I could think about is what you told me. The reason I do what I do is when I was 11-14, I was molested and I got more attention so I kept doing it. I've slept with over 40 men not trying to brag 'cause it's really not anything to brag about. I'm in a group home now and it's more structured so now I can learn new things to do instead of doing negative things. Well I hope you stay healthy and continue educating teens. You can say you saved one life mine. God love's you!

Love,
Jennifer

Dear Mrs. Rae Lewis,

Hello, my name is LaShay. On April 29, 1999, you spoke to a group of teenagers; I was in the audience that day.

First off I would like to say "Thank You". On that day you gave me so much hope, inspiration, and renewed self-being. Like you, my mother also has AIDS. I haven't told many people this because they don't understand it and think that it's contagious, and they think that it's a promiscuous person's disease. However, I know this is not always true. My mother contracted the disease by being an intravenous drug user.

My life has been very hard because of my mother. Throughout my childhood I was mentally, emotionally, and sexually abused. Then when things couldn't possibly get any worse, I was raped by my ex-boyfriend two months before my seventeenth birthday. All these things I blamed on my mother. Even the miscarriage, I had after being raped because she wasn't around, she was still doing drugs, and she had become a prostitute. I knew that she loved me and I just didn't love her back.

Now she's dying of cancer and AIDS and I want to tell her that I love her, but I don't know how. I don't want her to die thinking that I don't love her, yet I can't bring myself to say the words.

Then I heard you speak, and it was so spiritual and when I looked in your eyes I could see God. After you finished speaking, I went to the restroom and I cried. And it was so different because I never cry I always hold my feeling inside. The whole time I was in the restroom crying I was thinking. "Finally someone I can relate to and who understands what I'm going through." It was like a burden was lifted off of my shoulders, and when you hugged me it was like hugging an angel. This is why I say "Thank you."

With God's Blessings,
LaShay

As a speaker, this is the kind of the letter that you live for. My heart goes out to this young woman who has experienced so much pain. I sense that she is on her way to something better. The first step is letting go of the pain, and then the healing begins. For sure, her journey will be long; but through my story, she saw that she could make it. She saw that she was not alone. She found hope in my story. Along my journey, she found grace for herself and her mother. This makes my heart smile.

Dear Rae Lewis-Thornton,

Hello my name is Denise. I saw you when you were in Chattanooga, Tennessee. I was so motivated with your speech, that night I asked Jesus to come into my life. I am a 29-year-old, H.I.V. positive mother of three children. My children ages are 11, 10, and 7. I have two daughters and one son. The reason I'm writing this is because I felt people like "Us" stay in the closet. However, I guess too I was living a lie; Some how Mrs. Thornton your speech motivated me to the point, where I went home and told my family not only did I get saved but I'm going to be a HIV – AIDS 'active" speaker, just like you. I felt just listening I learned to not just get educated but also learn how to educate others. Rae life is to short so I feel God want me to go forward. I feel my knowledge about HIV can help educate and save others. On February 26, 1998, I was afraid to die. But now Rae, I feel that Jesus has told me; I've come to far already to be left in the mists of hell and not being saved. Therefore, today I'm on the Lords side. Friday and Saturday no more night clubs. I will not pretend ever again to fix something I cannot cure! My T-cell level today is 742. I have an undetectable viral load. Rae, I use to pretend to over look the non "cle-shas" of ever getting AIDS, however, I'm in doubt! I've only been positive for a year and a half. However Rae, I feel like it has been for some years now, I know or how should I put-it-with the arm's of "Jesus Christ" We will be here on earth till he is done with the both of us. Rae, I hope I can hear from you by telephone or letter you give me strength! I say to you Rae.

Thank you,
Denise

Dear Rae Lewis-Thornton,

Hello. My name is Bryan, from Crete Monee High School, and I'm the one who waited for about an hour to speak to you when you arrived back to the school after you came back from lunch. I wanted to tell you thanks for everything you said to the school and I. You really mean and are worth a lot to the school and I. So on my behalf, I would like to say thanks for speaking and please remember; you're always in our hearts, and minds. You mean a lot to everyone.

Sincerely yours,
Bryan

Dear Mrs. Rae Lewis-Thornton,

I recently had the pleasure of sitting in on one of your lectures. Well actually, I thought it less of a lecture, but more a conversation. It was as if you were talking to me personally. I must tell you that was one of the best AIDS education sessions I ever had seen. Believe me at my age you've seen plenty. Well let me tell you a bit about myself. My name is Stephanie, but I prefer to spell it Stefanie. I'm 14, and a freshmen in high school. But I'm going to be 15 on March 13th. I'm Hispanic and a typical teen. When you got up there, I really thought it was a joke. You're so healthy, so young and attractive. How could you have AIDS? I guess you can't judge a book by its cover. I consider you one of those lucky women. You have a wonderful husband to care for you. You change lives. You seem just like a normal person, but you're so wise for your age. Not degree wise, but rather profound wise. Almost as if you've lived a long experienced life in just a few short years. I admire you, your wisdom, and strength. You seem so strong, and I know God will guide you. He will see you through this. Please if you feel up to it, I would like to know you better. You seem so interesting to know.

You're in my prayers,
Stephanie

Dear Mrs. Thornton,

I just want to say that this is my 3rd time hearing you and I want to say that you are the most inspirational person that I have ever met. I love you so much. God Bless You! You have really blessed me.

Love you always,
Forever,
Infinitely,
Ayana

Rae,

From the depth of my heart, I want to extend a very personal thank-you for your dynamic delivery on last Wednesday at Metropolitan. Folks are still "Buzzin" about it!! YOUR ministry has helped to literally revolutionize heart and minds at our Church. Everyone, and I mean EVERYONE, wants you to come back. Hopefully, we can have you to return to talk solely to our youth. They need to hear your message.

May God continue to sustain you in your health and your ministry together.

With eternal gratitude,
Judi

Mrs. Rae Lewis-Thornton,

Hi! How are you doing? Hopefully fine. It's exactly 20 minutes after your speech. Between you and I your speech was the bomb! Seriously, when you said that you don't give a message to kids (students), that's wrong because you touched me in a way that nobody has ever touched me. You've really made me think about AIDS or any disease because life really is short so you should take what you can get. And when you first walked toward me and gave me a little smile, I felt so comfortable because I thought that I would feel uncomfortable but not because you have AIDS but because I've honestly never been so close to a person that have AIDS you are very, very, very attractive! I'm telling you if you weren't married you would most definitely have me under your belt. Your husband is a very lucky man! He's a nice guy. I respect him in all means!

Love ya!
Andre'

Dear Ms. Lewis,

So what's up? How's everything? I hope everything is fine. So how do you like this weather I think it sucks. But anyways I hope you're feeling great. After meeting you at school I felt sad. This was the first time that I met someone with AIDS. Now I know what it's like meeting someone and hearing you talk about it makes me think twice about sex in life. I think everyone needs some one to open their eyes and let them know that this can happen to you. Well I have a girlfriend her name is Geovonna. I've been with her for four years now. I told her everything. She wanted to meet you. Along with this letter I'm sending you a blessed scapular so you can wear around your neck. It's something so you could know that God is with you and that we will pray and have you close to our hearts. So please stay up and remember that you always have friends over in the north side so please take care.

I almost forgot, if you forgot my name and who I was, I'm Angel and I'm 18 and just graduated from Amundsen 3 weeks ago. I'm Mexican and I have a sister Marieta, a brother Johnny, dad Jesus and mom Lupe. I also have someone special in my life for my girlfriend Geovanna.

Here from you later,
Angel

Dear Rae,

I have been teaching a long time, and rarely have I seen my students as touched and penetrated by words of wisdom as I did when you came to speak to them at Evanston Township High School. They all said, "No one has ever talked to us like this before," and they have pondered and examined the things you told them over and over.

Thank you for your gift of wisdom and spirit that you were so unselfishly willing to share with us that day. Here are some words of thanks from my senior survey students I hope that the sincerity of there messages give you comfort and joy. You are in our thoughts and prayers daily. I feel so fortunate to have had the opportunity to bask in the beauty of your spirit.

Sincerely,
Linda

I am always happy to receive a letter from a teacher. Many times, the adults in the audience are a little upset because of my candor. They miss the point that I am there for the young people. This teacher got it. By the way, this particular school is my Alma Mater. The Assistant-Principal, Ms. Martin, who was a counselor when I attended Evanston Township High School (ETHS), reached out to me countless times and made sure that my ministry reached the current students. I am always grateful for those from my past who support my ministry. A repeated invite to one's Alma Mater is a privilege.

Dear Ms. Thornton,

I wanted to take this opportunity to thank you for coming and talking to my class at ETHS. I was very moved by your story and your courage to come out with it. After seeing a close friend of the family die from AIDS, I am very aware of the hurt and pain that accompanies this disease.

I only pray that if I'm ever faced with such a situation, I have half your courage. It's easy to be brave when the odds aren't against you, but when they are, it's very difficult. For a long time, I thought that there was no way AIDS could touch me, because I figured that I'd be responsible and careful. Now, I realize that as much as you say that ahead of time, when the moment presents itself, it's more difficult than one would think to remember to be responsible. I guess stories like yours have made me remember the importance of protection, because AIDS can happen to anyone. I only wish that more people realized that, instead of making fun of it or calling it a "fag disease." That kind of ignorance should not be tolerated, because it's ruining our world.

Thanks again! I know that your story made a difference for me and if that's worth anything, then you should feel good. Please know that you are in my prayers.

Sincerely,
Monica

Dear Rae,

Hi! My name is Chisa. I'm 15 years old. I was really touched by your story. You have a lot of guts to do what you are doing. I had a mom and my lil' sister die of AIDS. I go around, in school and try to get through to some people my age. Some hear me and some don't! But I don't care, I appreciate those who wanna listen. Well you know what really hurt me? I didn't know that my mom had AIDS until she was dying. She always, through words, hinted at me but I told her that we are all gonna die. I understand the period of denial, but I just didn't understand why couldn't she have told me. I know I should forget about that but it's hard. My lil' sis was just 7 when she died. Her death I took the hardest, by her being young and being my only sister. I really don't show my emotions through crying. I hold things inside. I know that's not good, but I just do. I don't like anyone to see me cry and say, "It's okay".

I don't like pity. Well anyways, I wish I could meet you one day. I want to go around the state and tell folks my story like you do but I don't know where to start. I've tried calling Montel, Carnie, Ricki and Rolanda but so far, they haven't called me. I have a friend who has full-blown AIDS that wants to talk with me. Like I said, I've tried getting through to people at school. I've even talked to my athletic group. Well I guess I better let you go! You take care, Rae!
God Bless You!!
Love, Chris

Dear Mrs. Thornton,

Hello. I know you may not remember who I am. My name is Kim and I am a junior at John Hersey High School in Arlington Heights, Illinois. Mrs. Esther Solar is my homeroom teacher. I am a member at Second Baptist Church in Evanston. I just wanted to write to tell you how much influence you had on me, personally, when I saw you speak at my school, church, and television, over a year ago. I never was one of those promiscuous teenage girls. As a matter of fact, I am a virgin and proud of it. Not only can I credit my parents and myself, but also I would like to thank you. I know this probably sounds funny to you. It might sound like I am thanking you for having AIDS, but I am not. I am thanking you for coming around when you did, and for being an excellent speaker, and for being an influential-beautiful-black-woman. I pray to God that I will one day have the strength and courage that you have.

I also wanted to write to tell you that I hope you are feeling fine. You sent me a Christmas picture of you and Kenny last Christmas. Believe it or not, that made my holiday more than any of the gifts I received. I still have that picture hanging in my locker, to this day. Every morning I see the picture and ask myself, "I wonder how Rae is doing?" Whenever someone comes to my locker, they asked, "Are those your parents?" That really makes me upset because I just assume that everyone who heard you speak in our school would remember you. So anyway, I truly hope you are feeling fine.

Best Wishes,
Kimberly

Dear Mrs. Thornton,

How are you, well I hope? I don't really know what to say to you. I don't want to say the wrong thing to you, and I don't want to hurt your feelings so all I'm going to say is I hope you are doing the things you have been doing and keep teaching the younger generation about the risk of having unprotected sex. I want kids to look up at you and say that was a strong ass woman, a woman with a mission, a woman with pride, and a woman with a hell of a lot of courage. Thank you for coming and talking to us about your experience with the outer world and what we have to do to stay alive in today's world.

Sincerely,
Michael

Dear Rae,

Hello, my name is Tammy Neely. I'm a junior at Winston Salem State University, Management Information System major. I'm in six clubs and organizations along with singing in the College Gospel Choir.

After returning to my room my suitemate asked me how was it. I told her she missed it. I tried to tell her everything that you said but it was impossible. Rae you had enlightened me about what your life's been like, I just said you missed it!

Even though its hours after your speech at Winston-Salem State University. I still had you on my mind. I was working on an assignment due Wednesday 4/3/96 but I can still smell your perfume on my clothes. I asked my roommate can she smell it and she said yes, was you that close to her. I said yes I gave her a hug (smiling)

I will keep you in my praises. That you may live to continue to tell your story, and educate everyone about AIDS. All ways remember that God will not put more on one than one can bear. I know it may seem as though God has. Just keep your spirits up as you have and keep educating others. I have enclosed a little something that I hope will make you happy in some way. Maybe you can buy some clothes or medicine with it.

P.S. This is 10% of my income taxes. I give to you. May God continue to bless you.

Love always, Tammy

Dear Ms. Thornton,

I came to hear you speak and you touched my soul.
Your words were uncomplicated and true.
Your wisdom older than you.
You showed you cared by exposing your soul.
You scared some, made some think, and got through to others.
While doing all this I could see the angel standing by your side.
Have no doubt God's love has a blinding affect as people share.
You are truly on a mission from God.
Let others think what they want, but know the truth, your words do matter.
Know that you will never be forgotten.
You will always be remembered.
Your words will live on in all that heard you speak.

With God's Love,
Mya

Dear Rae:

I am writing you in regard to your speaking engagement that took place at Cleveland State University Wednesday, March 22, 2000. I don't even know where to start. I do know that what I am about to say you've probably heard it a million times before, but you have an awesome testimony.

I admire you for your strength, your determination, your fight to keep going no matter how hard times have gotten for you in the past and maybe even now, but most of all I admire you for making God the center of your life. You cannot begin to know the impact your speech had on myself, although I have never experienced half the things you have, you opened my eyes and mind to things that I thought I would only read about in magazines, hear on the news or even read in a novel.

In your speech I heard you say you would debate about being a lifesaver. Well I know that does stand to be debated, but I feel you should debate no more because through Christ you have already saved lives you may not even realized you saved through your spoken words in person or your words in writing. Even if its only one person that will listen carefully and take heed to what you've said, you have at least saved one from having to face such a serious and mind blowing situation.

I am going to conclude by saying, the hug that I gave you at the end of the evening was in no way for pity because I don't pity you not one bit, I admire you to the utmost and that is exactly what that was for. I hope to see you again in Cleveland soon. It was more than a pleasure meeting you and I want you to know although we do not know each other; you have my support and most of all my friendship. You are a Gift from God.

Sincerely,
Angela

"You are a wonderful work...don't ever forget that. You were not hidden from me, for I created you. I have ordained all your days; they were written in my book before the beginning of time. My thoughts are precious to you...they are more than all grains of sand."
Psalms 139:14-18

Dear Ms. Lewis-Thornton:

My name is Sephena and I attended your presentation to Jack & Jill in Knox, TN, on Saturday, January 23rd. Although I am not a member of that organization, I am grateful they allowed me to attend.

For some reason, I felt this need to reach out and let you know the kind of impact you had on me. I realize that you encounter hundreds of people during your travels and remembering everyone who approached is impossible. Never-theless, I'm the woman who approached you, while you were sitting at the table in the hallway, and asked to shake the hand of the "bravest person I've ever met."

Let me put this in perspective. I've heard lots of people speak, share personal, painful experiences with groups, but for some reason, yours stood out. There was something about you – your aura – that went straight to my gut. You were no longer a stranger. In fact, it felt like I was listening to and hurting with a very close very dear friend. I can't explain this. Suffice it to say that if you ever need a friend in this part of the country, consider this an offer.

Respectfully,
Sephena

Dear Rae,

I hope you don't mind me calling you Rae. I feel like I know you. I listened to you speak at Cleveland State University on April 25, 1998. You really touched my heart and opened my eyes. God wanted me to hear what you had to say. My older brother has AIDS. He is a homosexual and contracted the virus through unprotected sex. I have been angry with my brother for his sexual preference and I guess I blame him for getting AIDS I don't tell people my brother is homosexual or that he has AIDS. Some of my closest friends that I have known for many years still don't know. They tell me how cute he is and asked if he is married or has a girlfriend. I just kind of laugh them off and tell them they don't want him. I don't like my mother to tell people because then they will know that my brother has AIDS.

My brother now, age 33 has not been a very responsible adult. He doesn't keep a job and started getting disability payments. When he tells me some days it's hard to get up and he just doesn't feel good. I tell him he is just lazy and doesn't want to work. He tells me I just don't understand. After listening to you, I realized I was wrong. I'm not sure what stage of the virus he is in. It has been about eight years since I found out he had the virus. I really don't know anything about what he has gone through. He has been in and out of the hospital. I never asked why. Right now I know more about how AIDS has affected your life than it has my own brother's life. My brother has become a drug addict since he has had AIDS. That has made it even harder for my family and I to deal with him. He has been clean for three months now and is looking much better. He is even gaining some weight. His doctor says he is doing better. I know he is dying but I try not to think about it. I want to enjoy the time we have together and be close like we were before he got HIV.

I want to thank you for being a blessing in my life. After listening to you, I am not angry with my brother any more. I am going to be more patient and understanding when he tells me he doesn't feel good. I still don't want people to know. That is something I have to work on... My mother is helping me with that because she doesn't have a problem telling anybody. You are a beautiful person and I thank God for you and your ministry. I love you.

Irene

"For God so loved the world, that he gave his only begotten Son, that whosoever believeth in him should not perish, but have everlasting life." John 3:16

Dear Ms. Lewis-Thornton:

Last night I attended your seminar at Guildfield Baptist Church and I was very moved by your riveting and touching story about your uphill battle with AIDS. To say that your message was most enlightening is an understatement!

What stood out foremost in your message - and this is my personal opinion, was how you continually gave God the glory and you did not speak out of bitterness, but spoke from the depths of your soul in a genuine desire to educate people about the realities of AIDS. Sister-girl, you are a very strong individual and I pray that God will continually strengthen you - your mind, body and soul.

Your message was raw and so very deep. It made me stop and think about the implications involved in today's dating scene. When you are watching two gorgeous individuals on a big movie screen taking casually about love and sex, with no mention of monogamy or marriage, and then in the next scene they end up in the sack and by the end of the movie the couple is living together, who stops to think about AIDS?! There's no mention of condoms and nobody talks about the history of the individual in the love scene, so of course you're (movie-goer) sitting in the movie thinking that you want to fall in love and you need a man etc. So, quite naturally when Mr. Goodbar breezes in you life looking like he just stepped out of EM, you ain't hardly thinking about whether or not he has AIDS. That's life in the 90's! (Not for me!)

However, your message brought reality to the doorstep of many of the listeners in the audience, particularly myself. It was evident by our expressions of shock and our tears that your words had hit home. It was definitely food for thought...

In addition, what I admire the most about you is that with all you've been through, and with only nine T-Cells, you somehow find the power to reach the people you need to reach and educate them about this deadly disease called AIDS.

Lastly, all last night I pondered on question "Lord why did she direct most of the answers to the question that were asked to me?" 'I don't specially look for guys that have Mercedez or Giorgio Armani suits, I don't really date; in fact I'm a virgin.' (22 years old; aren't you just proud of me?) You probably don't remember me but I was the one that asked you "How did you meet your husband?" And I was sitting on the second row to your right. Well anyway the Lord finally said Keisha, Rae is using you to get the message across to the other folks. So girls, you owe me one! (smile)

Oh, and by the way girlfriend that suit was "all of that!" and my size (smile). May God be with you, and thank you for opening my eyes to stark truth about AIDS.

P.S. - Think about writing a book (Bookseller). Consider it sold. Mmmmmmmmmmm

Sincerely,
Keisha

Dear Ms. Thornton,

Although we've never met, today, as you spoke, I recognized you. You stood and pirouetted before a somewhat complacent crowd of young students and adults. You see, they've heard many an AIDS victim before. They were prepared to be polite; they do care and would respond appropriately. But as your story unfolded, as you shared, as you revealed, as you dared, as you cared, you changed us—all of us, students, teachers, administrators, and parents. Don't misunderstand me; we would have cared about you if you had the personality of a cigar store Indian. But, now, after today, we all know that our souls have been touched.

As you stood inches away from me, I observed you swing from pain to laughter - "I'm a grandmother!" (This was in reference to your dog giving birth.) I couldn't help but react somewhat selfishly as I silently cursed God, our impotence, republiccans (Hey! Always republicans!), the list goes on. The world doesn't need one Rae Lewis Thornton: we need million's of you. We need your energy, commitment, and compassion... But then, you are giving that to us and, in so doing, the very best of you is being multiplied over and over. (Over sometimes blasé' students each felt that they were alone with you as you spoke and wrote about their dreams.) Kindness is simple, con-tagious and heroic.

I started this note to you by saying that I recognized you. I've been in the business of education for over twenty years. As the years pass and I meet new students and stretch as I endeavor to reach them, my love for my profession grows. Most days for me are a junkie's high—I teach!! I rejoice!! I know my trade and I recognize you fondly as a colleague. Teaching is all about change, compassion, riding roller coasters... Now, that's you. I welcome you to the ranks and I'm proud to stand with you. When you and I measure our life, even though my longevity surpasses yours, we'll share the same epitaph— TEACHER!

Sincerely,
Vikki

P.S. Magna cum laude!!! Summa cum laude!!!

Hello Mrs. Thornton,

My name is Demetria. I am a sophomore at the University of Arkansas-Pine Bluff maintaining a 3.8 GPA. I attended your presentation on September 18, 1995, and I must say you really touched my heart. Not only did you touch my heart but you also made an impact on my mind.

First, I must say I admire you (1) for your concern for other people; (2) for your courage to tell your story and the most personal things in/of your life; (3) for your outlook on life. In your presentation you said one thing that influenced my feeling of you. You said, "AIDS has control of my body, I have control of my spirit." I must commend you for your love and faith in God. At times I thought I had reasons to not look to God for everything; just listening to you, I remembered the scripture say, "In all things be content" - And I now strive much harder at this.

Your speech... answers... insights were overwhelmingly an inspiration to me and I want to help you "tell as many people as you can" while you can. My home church, Victory Missionary Baptist Church of Milwaukee, Wisconsin, where Dr. E.L Thomas, my father is the Pastor, really needs to hear your presentation. We have quite a few young ladies as well as young men who feel like having sex makes them a woman or a man but they aren't emotionally prepared for the consequences that may result; nor are they mentally, financially, or physically ready. It would mean a lot to me if they could hear your presentation. If you would consider speaking at my Church in Milwaukee or even making it a city-wide effort, would you please write me or my father and express your acceptance and conditions for accepting.

I know a lot of things you said to be true and I don't see why everyone has to make the mistake in order to learn from it; it seems to me that they should be able to learn from other people's mistakes. I think I have talked to them until I've turned blue in the face. I know you could make a good impact on them.

And just so that you know, I'll tell you honestly that this is my second year at UAPB and I have not had sex since I've been here; "you know trying to do that 'Christian' thang.

I pray your strength in the Lord. Thank you for the inspiration you gave me and the knowledge you shared with me. May God continue to bless you.

In the Name of Jesus, We Have the Victory,
Demetria

* * *

Dear Rae,

This is inexcusably late! Enclosed please find a paper written by one of my students, following your presentation at South Carolina State University late last fall. You really moved some souls that evening!

I thank the Lord for the time he has given you, and thank you for using it so unselfishly to try and educate and wake up people that might otherwise have not heard the truth.

May God continue to bless you and open the ears and hearts of all whom you meet.

Yours in Christ,
Ms Doucette

As I sat in the midst of the modestly crowded SHM, I sat and wondered what was about to happen. I assumed that this would be another boring seminar about AIDS, and the main reason why I was there was to write this paper. I have always considered myself to be a pretty knowledgeable person. I thought that I knew everything there was to know about AIDS from reading about it and listening to people on TV discusses it. During my freshman year, I even wrote a research paper about AIDS and the methods of prevention. Never in a million years did I expect to learn anything new from this forum. Not only did this woman educate me, she also struck in me a fear that I have never felt before. She literally touched the inner depths of my heart and pierced the seams of my soul.

The one thing that she kept saying that really stuck with me was "AIDS is deep!" Such a simple statement said so much. AIDS is a disease that is so deep that it touches and affects everyone. Unlike most institutions in this society, it discriminates against no one. You don't have to fit a certain description to get it. You don't have to be a certain sex, race, or religion. AIDS has no boundaries and no one is immune to its treachery, including me. I sat there almost paralyzed with anger, fear, and deep sadness as she fiercely rolled off her tongue over and over again, "I am dying!" Then I reminisced back to the magazine cover that created such a stir last year. The title said. "Facing AIDS: I'm young, I'm educated, I'm drug free, and I'm dying of AIDS." If one were to take her picture off and just read the headline, I would swear they could have been talking about me and many of my friends. Then it really hit home that AIDS does not discriminate. None of us are immune. "AIDS is deep!"

Maya Angelou said that human beings are more alike than they are different. Many of the things that Rae Lewis-Thornton said about life and relationships sound like scenes out of my own life and the lives of many of the people I associate with? We have all "played the fool."

I am very glad that I attended this program. Rae Lewis-Thornton is an oasis of strength and dignity. For her to share the things that she shared with us to help us save our own lives is an act of pure unselfishness and is evidence that God can manifest within the hearts of men (and women). She is indeed the strongest woman I have ever seen. At first I was offended by her abusive language, but I realized that those words were the only words appropriate to emphasize the deep abusiveness of AIDS. She has a right to be angry, because this disease seems to be so unfair.

Usually when any one person speaks for over an hour and a half, he or she loses my attention. I can honestly say she never lost my attention or my heart. The tears flooded my face at a very rapid rate. I sat there and mourned for a woman I have never met before in my life as if I had known her all my life. Suddenly her pain was my pain, her burden was my burden, and her story was a part of me. I thank God for her ministry and I thank you, Ms. Doucette for encouraging us to attend this program.

Anonymous

86

Dear Mrs. Thornton,

I am a freshman at the University of Illinois in Champaign Urbana. You spoke before a group of young people and I want you to know that I was really touched by your testimony. There are some things I'm going through in my life at this present moment, that I know I can't handle by my self. Thanks to you and a couple of people, I've decided to "step back and let God do it." You really inspired me tonight to make a change in my life that I should've made a long time ago. I'm involved in a relationship and I've decided that it's time to see if my relationship can stand the test. I've had sex at least once a month for the past 11 months and I've been telling myself and my boyfriend that it's time to stop but I haven't stopped yet. I believe that is because I've been trying to stop on my own. Since I've heard your testimony. I can truly say that "The battle is not mine, it's the Lords." So I've decided to let Him have His way in my life.

I thank you for the encouraging remarks you shared and I would like to give you a little encouragement, Also:

You can make it! These trials you're going through, God is going to show you just what to do. You can make it, yes you can! I don't care what's going wrong. God won't let it last too long.
You are not in this thing alone, you can make it!

(God won't let it last too long) This is a song I sing in my Church choir. I always sing it when I feel I can't go any further. I hope the words will

help give you strength and reassurance when you're at your lowest moments.

I thank you again for making a positive impact on my life.

Thanks again,
Love,
Tyra

Dear Rae Lewis Thornton,

Thank you for coming down to the school to talk to us about life having AIDS. I really do think you are a brave lady and damn good positive role model. When we have assemblies none of the people have ever attracted our or my attention like you. If you're able to come back, I hope that you do because I want to have a chance to give you a hug or shake your hand. By the way, tell your husband I said thanks for doing what I am going to do, stand by yours truly till there's no more movies.

Sincerely,
Dennis
I love you.

Mrs. Rae Lewis,

My name is Javonne and I am from Roberto Clement High School. I am writing you to <u>thank you</u>. If you only knew what I was going threw before I heard you speak. The things you said made me change my ways and maybe even my life.

I lost my mother at age 11 to breast cancer, which I watch eat away at her life for five years. After my mother passed my father changed he started using drugs. He started calling me lazy, stupid hoe; he even said that I would never do anything in life worth telling.

I started thinking everything he said was true. So I ran away at the age of 11 to a man that my aunt knew. He forced me to have sex with him. That's why I started having sex. I really didn't want to but sometimes they were giving me the attention with sex. A year ago I realized who I was. I thought about what I was doing. I moved in with my father's mother and she says just about the same thing. So I started doing good in school, joining clubs and teams in school just to try and prove my father and his mother wrong.

I decided to get goals and boundaries. I know what I want to be and I was not put on this earth to prove anything to anyone. That's why I love school so much. So one day I can be successful in life. Because I want too.

When I heard you for those last two days I got more confidence about myself. I know I may be keeping you to long but I just want to say Thank you one more time. You don't know how you have changed my spirit.

Always thinking of you, Jovanne

Rae,

Your powerful testimony touched my heart when you came to Mount Olive Baptist Church in Knoxville. May God continue to strengthen and use you to minister to others.

Yours In Christ,
Janice

Mrs. Thornton,

I hope you are feeling okay. You spoke at my high school. John Hersey High School in Arlington Heights, Illinois on April 17 last year. You probably don't remember me, but my name is Kim. I wrote an essay about you. I just wanted to let you know that you are truly an inspiration, and that we need more people like you to make the world aware of the disease. I also heard you on WGCI not too long ago. There was a lot of controversy at our school after you spoke. A lot of teachers didn't approve of your manner, and some even went so far as to say "... she sounded like she wasn't bothered by AIDS at all. That it's okay to have sex..." Those teachers really made me furious. The students really appreciated your down to earth persona. I really don't have a specific purpose for writing to you except to say stay as healthy as you can, keep up the good work and don't forget to pray. I've already decided that if I have a girl, her name will be Rae. Best wishes to you and your dogs.

Sincerely, Kim

Dear Rae,

I am writing to tell you that your speech at Howard was very moving and really hit home. I was one of the two girls who stayed after to talk to you after you were finished (at Howard University). I know you do a lot of speeches and can't necessarily remember faces, but I thought that would help you have some clue as to who I am. Anyway, like I said, I wanted to thank you for speaking so candidly and frankly to make us understand that this is real. I was very aware of the risks and I still was stupid enough to take chances. I haven't been diagnosed with anything as of yet (praise God), but I never know what my future holds. I do know that after hearing you speak, I have vowed to never take risks like that again (hopefully it's not too late). I always told myself that I wouldn't take chances, but when things heat up, things just happen, we all know that. But you made me reinforce the fact in my head that it only takes one and you never know who has it. I know you probably get many cards and letters, but I had to write you and let you know that you have really touched my heart and my soul. You are an inspiration to many but I know you are my personal hero who shows me that black women can really persevere and over come the many obstacles of life.

God bless you!
Sabrina
P.S. You are always in my prayers!

Dear Mrs. Lewis-Thornton,

Upon recently hearing you speak at Jack & Jill of America Inc. National Teen Summit in Oakbrook, IL. I was compelled to write you a letter. When I first thought of writing this letter I was uncertain what to say, whether to say thank you for sharing your story or thanks for educating our minds was the question I asked myself. It occurred to me that thank you might not be the correct or even necessary word to sum up what your speech meant to me. I recall the day I was first introduced to Rae Lewis-Thornton, December of 1994 when Essence magazine arrived at my doorstep. I immediately grabbed it to see what interesting stories it would have regarding hair and make-up. However the cover took me by shock!!! The words "I'm young, I'm educated, I'm drug-free, and I'm dying of AIDS" immediately took me by surprise. I was certain this beautiful African-American woman could not be infected with HIV or even have AIDS. I read every word of your story engrossed, intrigued and even poised the question to myself "Could this happen to me"? I had to re-read certain parts of the story and even refer to my mother at times to help me understand some things. You see the day your Essence article arrived at my doorstep I was only 13. I had never truly understood HIV or AIDS and it wasn't until many notable figures addressed the fact they had it that I even began paying serious attention. Now I guess you could say I am in the prime of my life 16 years old high school honor student. I even have the better things in life DKNY, Ralph Lauren and Nautical clothes fill my closet. However all the material-istic things in the world could never have as grave an impact as your story and the words you speak. When I leaned of your presence at our National Conference I was quite surprised as well as overjoyed. I was surprised because I know how candidly you speak and wondered if our ultra conservative Jack & Jill mothers knew that. I was overjoyed that I would finally have the opportunity to hear you speak and tell the Rae Lewis-Thornton story. Upon your entrance in the room I was pretty sure many of the teens had no clue who you were. I say this arrogantly because sometimes our world does not go as far as Contempo Casual or Neiman Marcus. However, as I watched you confidently walk down those stairs and introduce yourself I saw the room become quiet and all attention focused on you. As I listened to your story, I thought in my head if I was to ever be faced with a challenge like this one I hope I can be just like her. I guess my main purpose in writing this letter is to say thank-you for educating and enlightening Jack & Jill teens of America everywhere. From now on when we hear your name in all the various cities we live in we can all recall the experience of hearing your words. I feel fortunate enough to live in the same city as you quite possibly your strength will be passed threw the city air. I am also writing this letter to inquire if there is an opportunity for a 16-year-old student to volunteer at the Rae Lewis-Thornton Foundation. I would feel privileged to work with you and your foundation members.

You have made a memorable mark on my life and I wish you the best of luck. Once again, thank-you so much for telling your story for all to hear.

Sincerely,
Maya

Dear Rae,

I had the opportunity to attend your forum on December 1ˢᵗ at FAMU. At the time, I had a class and was unable to speak to you at the end. I just wanted to express my gratitude to you for being honest about AIDS and for having the courage to speak about your afflictions to our student body.

I entered Florida A.M. University in 1991, at the age of 18. I was a virgin then, and even though I've come across some trying times, I am still a virgin. Although at times it's not easy, I realize that in our society, it's difficult to know all aspects of a person romantically and sexually. While abstinence will not be a permanent state of mind, at this point in my life it is the best alternative.

Thank you and God bless you,
Crystal

* * *

Karen Townsend and I go way back. We worked together on Social Justice Issues in the mid-eighties. We had lost contact for years. After I went public with my illness, she tracked me down. She has been one of the few people from my past political days that have truly embraced my work around HIV. She has ensured that my message is heard by securing me as a speaker for Wright State University. She continually supports my ministry. I was delighted to receive these stories from her students.

I had heard so much about this dynamic lady, from my instructor Mrs. Townsend, which she almost sounded to good to be true. Throughout the week, I heard of her passion for life and her promise to never give up. I went to the Black Student Union meeting and heard her name, I walked down hallways and saw her picture and I finally said to my self "Dang. She must really have something to say." Her name was Rae Lewis-Thornton and she was "Living with Aids."

Rae Lewis-Thornton and my instructor had been good friends over the years and had been planning her visit to Wright State University. She had also been preparing for a special visit tour UD 101 class. Mrs. Thornton was coming to our class to speak and Mrs. Townsend wanted us to be ready, so she played a tape of ABC's Nightline in order to familiarize the class with Rae's story. As I listened to Ted Koppel I heard prejudged ideas on how she should look, his amazement at how she did look and his surprise at how strong and able she was. Nevertheless, I listened to her and her thoughts on her appearance and well-being. I watched her motivate and stimulate audiences of all different kinds, and even though I couldn't empathize, I could sympathize. I heard her message, saw her struggle and felt her pain. After the video, I had various impressions of Rae. Among them were ones of courage, strength and perseverance. I was definitely ready to meet this truly wonderful and blessed woman.

The day finally came and, of course, our class was too excited. We had an opportunity no one else had. We could talk to Rae one on one. As I sat in class I heard the story of how she contracted the virus, how she dealt with it and how she now lives with it. I didn't, however, hear any hurt, anger or resentment in her voice. Her positive attitude made me look at my life and realize how strong a person would have to be to arrive at the point she's at. I was even more impressed with her story this time because it was real. She was real, her story was real, and the reality of both were sitting right in front of my face.

That same day she spoke to an audience in our Medical Science building. I brought my mother and my younger sister so they could witness what I had. I was deeply touched when I heard her speak and I kept thinking to myself: "If only I had heard her speak a couple of years ago. I might not have made some of the decisions I have. However, as I kept listening, I heard her telling me that it's never too late to start making "intelligent decisions." At that very moment, I did just that. I now realize that I am the only one who is going to protect and care for me.

Hearing Rae Lewis-Thornton speak was a wonderful, worthwhile and memorable experience. She is a very unique woman who was been blessed enough to bring her story to us. However, we are just as blessed, if not more, to be able to hear it. After feeling the emotional and physical impact of her story, I can truly say that she is my motivation and she is why I will start making my own "Intelligent Decision."

By Keysha

"Rae's Story"
By Ra Shanita

I did not want to go to class. I especially did not want to listen to someone's struggle with AIDS. My first exact thoughts were, "Okay, I struggling with Biology 112." I also knew that if I went to class, some of my heart – strings would be plucked and pulled. This would cause me to have violent and intense fits of sobs and tears. I just could not handle it.

Handle it. I thought that if I were to receive a death sentence like AIDS, I would jump off a very, very high building. I would not be able to handle the suffering. I would not handle the pain. I would not, could not handle an incurable, deadly virus. That is when I walked through the door for class. That is when I saw her.

Rae Lewis-Thornton was dressed casually in a black, long sleeve silk shirt that engulfed her slender torso. She was wearing a pair of jeans and still possessed an air of elegance. In fact, just by looking at her I knew there was something peculiar about her. I liked that.

Rae told my class her story. It was blunt and to the point. As I reflect back to everything she said, I can only remember bits and pieces. It is as if I heard her in a dream. Maybe it was a nightmare. I could not remember what she said, but I definitely felt what she said. I could feel her trying to make me understand. Every gut – wrenching point was clear, concise, and free of doubt. I fought back tear after tear. I did not cry.

I thank God for her. No one can truly realize the impact Rae had on me. I could not stop reflecting on my life. I was angry, scared and sometimes a little light-hearted. I listened attentively as I prayed to God. I thanked Him for this warrior; this divine intervention He placed before me. I did not cry.

"Save yourself." Those were Rae Lewis-Thornton's final words. Although I was one of many faces, it seemed as if she was talking to only me. Her advice was almost a whisper. These two words drifted to me. Me. It was like the calm before the storm – cold, scary, and quiet. I did not cry.

When I went home, I closed my door and I looked around my room. I saw my roommate's empty bed. I saw the picture of my current boyfriend hugging me before we went to my senior prom. I saw my Wright State University shirt on the floor. I saw the telephone. I saw the window cracked open and felt a cool breeze from it. It was not a dream. It was not a nightmare. It was real. I cried.

"And God shall wipe away all tears from their eyes; and there shall be no more death, neither sorrow, nor crying, neither shall there be any more pain: for the former things are passed away."
Revelation 21:4

Silent Wonder
By Nicole

I'm not really sure where I was or what I was doing when I heard the phrase, "Rae Lewis Thornton...living with AIDS." My first thought was DAMN! I've heard that name before but where? As the talk continued, I heard them say, "Rae... coming to talk at Wright State University." "Oh my God!" "Rae is coming here!" I thought. I could feel a mixture of anticipation, excitement and fear slowly rising inside of me. When? Where? Were questions swarming through my head. Those questions were soon answered.

On Monday, October 14, our UD 101 class began our discussion on "Let's talk about Sex, Part 1." As our instructor Mrs. Townsend stood in front of us, she began telling a story. A story none of us knew. It turns out that Mrs. Townsend and Rae had met some years ago. As time went on, distance and their own lives pulled them apart. It wasn't until Rae made the cover of Essence that Mrs. Townsend found out how her friend was doing – and she wasn't doing well. Rae had AIDS. Mrs. Townsend continued with her story and several minutes later she put in a videotape of the story ABC's Nightline did on her. I was surprised to see the full figured woman with a beautiful face that was on the cover then, become a slim trim, petite woman now – one of the signs that she was sick. Nonetheless, she was still beautiful. Living her life to the fullest every single day as if it is her last brought me to tears, the uncertainty, the not knowing. You would never know she had AIDS. That phrase sounds all too familiar. As the tape played on I was shocked by how brutally honest she was, both to the young and old. Her graphicness made me feel uncomfortable at first and sometimes sit back and gasp. But the more I listened to her talk, the more I realized that she had to be honest and uncensored to truly reach people and make them

99

understand that having this disease is much worse than you can tell just by looking at her. How could such a captivating voice come from such a fragile person? As I watched on in awe, I realized she was much stronger than she looks. To be so sick and yet still find the courage and strength to carry on with a hectic schedule of tour dates, radio and television appearances, and never showing how sick or tired she just amazed me. Even when she was hospitalized, I couldn't tell how sick she really was.

Then the day finally came when I got a chance to meet her. It was Wednesday, October 16 and she came to talk to our class before her evening forum. It took her a few minutes before she came in the room to talk to us because a local news crew was interviewing her. Then she walked in. There she stood – up close and personal. I looked her over carefully, nothing noticeable to the naked eye of her having the disease. She began talking, her tone softer than the way her voice is projected by the microphone. Our talk was intimate and uncensored with her leaving the discussion up to us to take it where we wanted it to go. To my surprise, she stated that "no question was too personal." We discussed her life, her living and dying with the disease, prevention methods, and most importantly reexamining our future goals. Sure, we have all heard the speeches about focusing on what is important in life like family and education, but sometimes it takes hearing it from someone who worked hard to get what she's got only now to have it not mean a damn thing – because she is dying. I left class that day feeling saddened yet having a sense of renewal. The realization of what is truly important came over me.

Seeing Rae later on that night at the forum, it was like looking at the video only with one difference, I was there. She shared most of the same things she had shared with us and things I didn't know. Although it was getting late and I know she was tired from her long day (because I was) she

100

found the strength to go on. DAMN! What a remarkable woman! After it was all said and done, I stood in a long line for her autograph and when I reached the front a wave of guilt came over me. Why? Looking into her face, her eyes, her tired eyes, made me feel that guilt. Here I was only caring about getting what I wanted all the while taking away precious minutes from her life. She managed a smile beneath the exhausted expression on her face and graciously signed my program. I walk away feeling guilty but indeed happy that I had met someone who no doubt had an impact on my life and yet wondering – Will I ever see her again? Will she be alive?

* * *

The following letters are from students who heard me speak at my first HIV Seminar at Bowen High School in Chicago. These young people were incredible. I conducted three workshops for a total of two days. After the first workshop, students began "skipping" class to hear me speak over and over. I left this school clear that God had a new purpose for me. Three weeks later, I quit my job and launched a new career and my ministry. It did not matter that I had no brochure and no other speaking engagements arranged. I just stepped out on faith and God did the rest. It has been ten years and I still do not have a brochure, but God has kept the speaking engagements coming and the ministry flowing.

These young people are an example of the level of honesty and integrity you get from youthfulness. There is a rawness in their honesty that sometimes cut. I learned from day one to appreciate this rawness. If you come straight with them, they will come straight with you. I have received some criticism over the years for my candor with young people. Of course the criticism is never from them. They are clear; it is the grown folks who are not. I believe if you give young people intelligent information about sex and the impact that sex will have on their life, they will make intelligent choices.

These letters illustrate their desire to know the truth. It also shows their humanity. I will always be grateful to Bowen High School and Ms. Willia Johnson for giving me my first chance.

*I was scared because she said it all of a sudden.
I would like to thank you because you stopped me
from having sex last night with my girlfriend.
I think you should speak more because it was real
brave of you to speak at Bowen.*

*May God Bless You!!
Mathus*

*I was scared of her; I wouldn't touch her with a
ten-foot pole. But I hope she gets better.*

Anonymous

Dear Ms. Lewis,

*I have to admit I wasn't really listening to you
at first. But when you came out and said that
you had AIDS. I stopped clowning around and I
began to listen to you. I must say you shocked me
and you filled me with knowledge of things that I
didn't know. I enjoyed your presentation, and I
hope you continue to keep up the good work you
put an impact on people's mind.*

*Sincerely,
Dianna*

Dear Rae Lewis,

Hi. How have you been? Healthy, I hope. People say that I'm sort of a funny boy, well right now I don't feel so much like laughing. Rae, sometimes when I go to one of them places where some adult is talking about AIDS. I always ask if they have AIDS and they say no. When I heard you say you had AIDS, I turned my head with my mouth opened like some fool for like half an hour. All I could do is pay attention to every word you said. Anyway all I want to say is I hope you keep healthy 'cause that's the only way you'll survive.

Sincerely your friend,
Eduardo

Dear Ms. Lewis:

I'm sorry to hear that you have AIDS, I think it takes lots of guts to go in front of a lot of people and talk about AIDS and tell people that you have AIDS. You showed me and many other people that anybody can get AIDS. Thank you for coming to our school I hope you visit again.

Sincerely,
Luis

Dear Ms. Lewis,

   I really enjoyed you telling us about AIDS. I did learn more than I knew. I use to think that you could catch AIDS by eating or drinking after someone with the virus. But now I understand more about it. I appreciate you coming and I'm going to try to learn more about AIDS.

Sincerely yours,
Shavaze

PART THREE

TO MY SURPRISE

REFLECTION: TO MY SURPRISE

$\mathcal{M}$any times, I receive letters from people that surprise me. It may be two, three and even five years after someone heard me speak. They write to tell me that I have been in their prayers or that they were just thinking about me. Sometimes, it is an old classmate or a buddy from my political days. Other times, it is someone who heard me on the radio or saw me on a news show such as <u>Nightline</u> or a talk show such as, The Oprah Winfrey Show. Then there are those who have read one of the countless magazine articles that have featured my story such as, *Ebony* and *Black Excellence*. There are those who have read every article that has been written on me. I do have some fans. I received these letters and they touched me in so many different ways. I have kept every letter ever sent. I realized in some regard that people chronicle my life through the letters they send me. My life is definitely reflected in these lines.

Sista Rae,

Thank you very much for being strong for us. Thank your very much for overcoming the pain to save us. Save our lives.

I'm not sure if you know this or not but you have made a difference in the lives of many young people.

Last year you spoke at the University of Illinois in Champaign. Your words echoed across the campus long after you left. Many of the young women in my life took the challenge you offered and many found out you were right.

I have gained great inspiration and respect (and love) for you and I pray that you will stay strong in the Lord (as you are) and continue your journey with pride and strength.

Thank you sistah,
Your sistah Yelene

Yelene is referring to the challenge I make to college campuses across the country. I ask young ladies not to have sex with their boyfriends, from the day that I spoke until after spring break. This time of celibacy usually ranges from one week to two months. During this period, they are to see if their boyfriends will respect their choice not to have sex. If he cannot or will not respect this choice of celibacy, it could be an indication of a shallow foundation of ones relationship. If he flunks, I ask young ladies to ask themselves, if they want someone in their life that does not respect the choices they make about their body and life? Take the challenge.

Dear Rae,

Let me preface this letter by stating that I've never written to a stranger before, but I was so compelled by your story that I had to.

Your obvious strength and courage goes without saying, but I think it's your brutal honesty that grabs people by the collar and says, "wake up!"

In 1989, I lost a dear friend to ARC. Unfortunately at that time the stigma of having AIDS was so strong that she pushed everyone but her immediate family away. I didn't even know that she died from AIDS until a year after her death. I've always felt so sad, that she felt that she couldn't share with me. I would like to offer you the support that I couldn't give Barbara. When you're sick and scared at 2 am, take it out and read this letter and I hope it will act as a mental hug. Also know that all the positive energy that is gone out will come back to you ten fold. The way that you're unselfishly relate to the people you speak with, will leave a productive legacy. In closing, I want to thank you for compelling me to write this letter. I will keep you in my hopes and prayers.

Sincerely,
Maggie

Rae,

Don't let no one or nothing steal your joy!

Keep on Livin',
Tasha

Dear Ms. Thornton:

After seeing your picture in Wednesday, September 6th Defender, I thought I would drop you a line just to say how proud I am of you. Your courage and positive image is to be commended.

Continued success on all your future endeavors.

Sincerely,
David

David Orr is a friend from my political days. He is one of the most politically correct men that I know. At the time this letter was sent, he was and remains the Clerk of Cook County in Illinois. He has always been on the forefront fighting for the rights of the left out and the locked out. I was both surprised and delighted to receive from him this note. It was great to know that some of those I worked with in politics support my work around HIV/AIDS.

Dear Rae,

I got your address from the E.T.H.S alumni directory. You probably don't remember me, I was a few years (2) behind you in high school but you may remember my brother David who graduated the same year as you.

Since I read your story in Essence, you have been on my mind. My heart goes out to you, and I wanted to extend my support for your struggle. As I read your story. I found your words to be both powerful an educational. I'm sure there are thousands of other women who were equally moved. Best of luck to you in your future endeavors! You'll be in my thoughts and prayers!

Sincerely,
Patrice

Life is funny, I did not remember Patrice, but I did remember her brother David. He was the cutest guy in the 7th and 8th grade class at Chute Middle School, Evanston, Illinois. I was very surprised to receive this letter from his sister. Life is interesting because David, now a State Representative in Illinois, and his wife, Donna, are among my circle of friends. I never imagined that his path would cross mine, years after junior high and high school. Nonetheless, receiving this letter from a former classmate truly touched me.

Dear Mrs. Thornton,

I know you are probably thinking, "who is this person." My name is Cynthia and I am in the 8th grade. I attend Hayes Middle School. Every Thursday a lady comes to our Social Studies class and teaches us about our health. She showed us a video about you going to different schools talking about your AIDS (symptoms). Oh, the lady that teaches us about our health name is Mrs. Shine. Mrs. Shine gave us the address where we can send you a Christmas card without you not knowing who I am. I hope this card brings a smile on your face. Well, I guess I will close by saying, "HAVE A MERRY CHRISTMAS."

Cynthia

Hello Rae,

I would like to know what kind of advice would you give a kid like me, who lost 3 friends, my uncle and 2 good friends to HIV and AIDS?

Jonathon

P.S. I think you are a beautiful and sophisticated women. May God be with you.

I was very very happy to receive these two letters among others, as a result of the news reports I did on WBBM-TV about HIV/AIDS. It was a great experiment. WBBM-TV Chicago hired me as a contributing editor to do a series of first person stories on my life living with HIV. I sat anchor each night the stories aired in an eight-part series. The reports had a huge impact on Chicago viewers. Many were glued to the 10:00 o'clock news to see what part of my journey I would share next. We did stories on AIDS and dating, AIDS and support systems, disclosure, relationships, AIDS and women, AIDS and teens, AIDS in the workplace and finances, to name a few. We gave Chicago viewers an up-close look at what it is like to live with HIV/AIDS. People would come up to me on the streets just to talk about the stories. Sometimes, people would come up to me on the streets and buy me lunch. They remembered when I said that proud people never ask. Other times, they would stop me in the store and ask if I had taken my medication. The series gave people a realistic look at HIV. I won an Emmy Award for those reports. The team at CBS was great. Edie Kasten and Mary Ann Childers will always be among my friends.

Dear Mrs. Lewis-Thornton:

I have always considered AIDS and HIV a serious disease. I have always paid attention to the information about safe sex and protecting myself from the disease and other conditions. My mother raised me to understand the importance of protecting myself once I decided to be sexually active.

When my friends and I would host AIDS awareness programs at our university, and the programmer would ask the question, "How many of you know someone who is HIV positive or who has AIDS?" many of our friends would raise their hands, but my friend and I would feel blessed that we were able to keep our hands in our laps, until recently.

A few months ago my friend found out that the reason she hadn't seen a friend of hers around school for such a long time was that she had been hospitalized because she has AIDS and that she had contracted an AIDS related illness. For a while she was living with such a terrible disease. My friend and I discussed how we felt, how her friend was feeling, and how blessed we truly were. Then, we both realized that now we couldn't keep our hands in our laps because now we both knew someone who was HIV positive!

As college students we were always curious about articles and information on the disease because being informed is one of the reasons we went to college. But since we have found out about this friend we have been briefing each other with stories relating to AIDS and people who are living with AIDS, then we came upon your story in ESSENCE.

We, the members of the Black Student Union, discussed your story in detail during our rap sessions because we know how under educated our people are in many areas but especially about HIV. We wondered silly things like, "how could she be infected, she's so pretty", or "she looks so smart how could she have done something so dumb?" But once we got over the initial shock, we realized just how important this subject was.

We realized that HIV doesn't care how cute you are and that calling someone dumb for bad judgments many years ago is not going to change the fact that you, and unfortunately many others, have this disease. What we finally realized what was really important was to find out how to stop the spread of the disease and making the lives of the ones who already have it as normal and as comfortable as possible.

Recently, I found out my cousin has AIDS and is in a comma (as of this writing he has lost his battle). It was not a surprise to me or many of my family members because we were aware of his past lifestyle, but that does not change the feelings I have for him and his family. I am actually glad that I was able to see him one last time, this past summer, like he use·to be.

I am telling you all of this because after reading your story and seeing your reports on channel 2. I have grown to admire you and your strength. I don't think I have been as brave as you were and still are to tell millions of people your story. I'm glad to see that you are telling young brothers and sisters the hard, true, facts about HIV and what it means. So many of them need guidance in many areas especially on issues concerning their health. I will continue to watch your segments and pray that you continue to be blessed with the love of your friends and family throughout your illness. I will encourage my friends to watch hoping that they will learn from your reports and spread the knowledge through words or through action!

Good Luck Rae! I wish you Well!
Sincerely,
Danielle

Dear Rae,

I am a thirteen-year-old female who has been watching your special on channel 2 news. I think that you send a powerful message to all people by appearing on television and telling your own story of living with A.I.D.S. It shows everyone that a person who has this syndrome looks, acts, and has feelings just as all other human beings do. I do not live with the disease or it's virus, but I agree that those who do should be treated just the same as all other people are. Thank you for taking the time to read my letter. Please keep on educating others about the disease and its' virus. I appreciate, the fact that you are doing this to help others. I will continue to watch you on television. Thanks again.

Sincerely,
Kornacker

* * *

Mr. Murphy was my seventh grade homeroom teacher. I first entered Chute Middle School in the 7th grade. My mother and I moved from the Southside of Chicago to the suburbs of Evanston. Mama was a maid at the Evanston Inn and she wanted to be closer to her job. This was one of the best decisions that my mother made. It had a profound impact on my life. When I entered Chute Middle School, my reading level was far below the 7th grade level. Mr. Murphy recognized my ability and was responsible for getting me tutors to improve my reading comprehension. Truly, it is teachers like Mr. Murphy who makes the difference. You know the rest of the story. I graduated from college with honors and my graduate level studies have all been met with equal zeal. I am grateful for Mr. Murphy.

I was honored that he arranged for me to speak at the school where he at the time was vice-principal. I was even more surprised when he jolted me a note. Teachers really are special people.

Words can never express how deeply your statements at the King Lab assembly affected me, I'm only sorry that it was such a bittersweet occurrence that connected us again. The things that you said were what a teacher lives for. Whatever role I played in any school, essentially I will always be a teacher. Your message to our students was powerful as well as most courageous on your part. My thoughts and prayers are with you.

Fondly,
Jerry

Dear Mrs. Rae Lewis-Thornton,

Recently upon reading your article in the December 1994 edition of Essence I became very impressed with you as a person, not just a victim of Aids, but as a human being. I read your story Facing Aids over and over trying to get a better understanding and visualize what you are going through. I'm not a victim of Aids but I have had love ones fall victim to this dreadful epidemic. Mrs. Thornton, the reason I'm writing you is to let you know how much I admire you and look up to you for what you have accomplished and worked so hard to possess while combating the disease. I can't stop thinking and praying for you since I finally had a chance to grace your presence at a recent graduation and you looked more stunning in person as well as the cover of the well publicized magazine.

As you stood at the podium to except the "Educator of the Decade" award at Kennedy-King graduation, I felt so much compassion in my heart that at that moment tears streamed down my face as you spoke on how you struggled so hard to accomplish and achieve in life and you didn't want your achievements to go down in vain. Well Mrs. Thornton, I'm here to let you know that your hard work and success will not go down in vain. With the help of "Our Lord Jesus Christ" and our Compassionate and Caring hearts we should be able to triumph and conquer the dreadful disease. Mrs. Rae Lewis-Thornton the Lord uses us in many ways and this is my calling to reach out to our youth as well as the world to explain once again that this epidemic among us does not discriminate and that there is life beyond this cynical world.

Love,
Saleme
A true friend and admire.

Dear Rae,

I just wanted to send a letter of encouragement to let you know that God loves you. I heard you speak at a singles conference at my Church, Eastern Star, a long time ago and you really blessed me. I know God is really using you and going to bless you for all the many people set free through your willingness to allow God to speak through you. I just wanted to tell you thanks for being real! Have lunch on me!

Be Blessed
Tamara

* * *

As you may guest, I get hundreds of letters from people who are trying to "save" me. Yes, I get more Jehovah Witness' tracts than anyone. I also get tapes, books and sometimes prayer cloths that will heal me. I have to be honest; sometimes, I am offended. At times, I have even been horrified. But mostly, the letters are well received. I understand at the end of the day, people only want to help. Sharing the Gospel is one clear way to help someone. I know this best because I share the Gospel of Jesus Christ every chance I get.

This letter is one of those well received. She heard me on the radio and sent these words of encouragements.

Dear Rae:

I would like to share with you a few verses that were shared with me. I know you probably are familiar with every verse in the Bible, but I'm doing this from the heart because I know that God is good.

I sit and think about the things. I'm going through personally and it's nothing compared to your fight of AIDS and of making people aware of the disease. I just wish you the best of luck in getting your point across to young people (African-American, White Hispanic, etc.) and fighting this disease. You are a true blessing and I'm pretty sure you never felt that telling people about a deadly disease would be a part of your life but since it is, continue to hold on to God's hand. The 23rd Psalm is more than just a verse, or verses it's a reliever when you feel discouraged and I just ask you to carry it in your heart and everything will be all right.

You are one of God's chosen, I know it's hard to believe this is the way but everyone has something they must do to leave a lasting impact here in the world. May God bless you and your husband and I will keep you in my prayers as well as others Aids victims.

The Lord is My shepherd; I shall not want.
He maketh me to lie down in green pastures;
he leadth me beside the still waters.
He restoreth my soul he leadth me
in the paths of righteousness for his name's sake.
Yea, though I walk through the valley of the
shadow of death,
I will fear no evil: for thou art with me thy rod
and thy staff they comfort me.
Thou preparest a table before me in the presence
of mine enemies
thou anointest my head with oil: my cup runneth
over.
Surely goodness and mercy shall follow me
all the days of my life: and I will
dwell in the house of the Lord forever. Amen.

Dear Mrs. Thornton:

Hello! My name is April. I am 16 years old, a rising senior at Faith Academy School of Excellence is Norfolk, Virginia. My school is an all African-American school, founded by Bishop Barbara M. Amos pastor of Faith Deliverance Christian Center. I am writing to you to tell you how encouraged I was when I read your story is the November/December issue of Black Excellence and to see you on the Oprah Winfrey Show.

Being a young African-American female myself I admire your strength and courage to battle it out and fight this disease that has affected so many of our people. I have never really been personally affected by this disease or come in contact with anyone who has it. This is one reason why I am writing this letter to you.

I would like to be in contact with you and to learn about your everyday fight with AIDS. I also wanted to ask you to come to my Church one day and speak. I am asking you to write me back with a response to this letter. Thank you for your time!

Sincerely,
April

* * *

Although *Essence* magazine helped to launch my ministry nation-wide, *Ebony* magazine was the first national publication to feature me in an article about HIV/AIDS. In April 1994, I appeared in an article about the impact HIV/AIDS has had on heterosexual women in the African-American Community. Over the years, *Ebony* has been very supportive of my work around HIV/AIDS, featuring my story in both *Jet* and *Ebony* magazines. Additionally, *Ebony* continues to address AIDS in the African-American Community. I am grateful for their fidelity.

It is interesting to me that many friends from my past have actually written me as a result of an article that they read in *Ebony*. These are some of the letters from individuals who read an *Ebony* article featuring my story.

Dear Rae,

When I read the article in Ebony (April '94)—I had to write. I am your former SIU roommate's sister. The last time you and I saw each other was at Bally's on 25 E. Randolph about a year ago.

You can't imagine the shock I had when I saw you in the article. I am truly sorry to hear about your contacting AIDS.

I just wanted you to know that someone's thinking about you and wishing you the best.

Take care,
Valerie

Dear Ms. Lewis,

I recently read the article about you in Ebony Magazine concerning AIDS and heterosexual African American Women.

The AIDS virus is a serious disease that is impacting society. My heart goes out to you and others who are dealing with this affliction. Your speaking out about your experiences will hopefully touch someone else's life and make them more aware and to educate them. I commend you for your diligent efforts and encourage you to continue the fight against AIDS.

Sincerely,
Tina

Hey Rae,

I first found out about your illness, when I read, I believe the April or May Publication of Ebony magazine. I was very saddened and hurt. So many people particularly African-American people have contracted this dreadful disease. Rae, you're such a wonderful person, and committed person to our struggle. But this disease really doesn't care about the character of the individual, or about whether you're nice, mean, attractive, unattractive, young or old.

Rae, working with you in past campaigns or just in our overall struggle, I've gained a lot of respect and admiration for you. You're very bright, committed, and sincere individual.

It felt extremely good to see you at PUSH about a month ago. You look so good and good to see you with such a positive attitude.

Rae, I hope and pray that before this illness overcomes you completely, a cure is found. I feel very confident that you will make it. I feel confident that a cure will be found soon, so that all of our people and other people around the world, with the illness, will be restored back to good health, especially you.

Love you,
J.J.

Dear Rae,

As Salaam Alaikum! (Peace Be Unto You)
I pray Allah (God) this letter finds you in wonderful spirits and preserve health. It was a pleasure speaking with you two weeks ago. I was pleasantly relieved to hear your spirits so high and your life so filled with purpose and of course, the news of your upcoming wedding was ad-ditional pleasure.

When I read in Ebony about your condition, my heart was burdened because I remembered you from the campaign of Reverend Jackson – as you at that time were a tremendous inspiration to me as a young person that had committed your life to the struggle of our people at such an early age. I have no doubt that seeing you in your commitment in 1984 is part of the reason that I am still in the struggle today.

I know that politics was your interest, but we know that Allah works in mysterious ways. As Muslims, we believe that nothing happens except by the permission of Allah, so undoubtedly Allah has a bigger mission for you in mind and if you can elevate the is bigger and more noble work than politics. For that saves the lives of our people, politics is about taking from the people.

Your work today is about giving a more precious gift – life. Also as Muslims, we believe that Allah never places a burden upon a person that they are not made to bear. You are a strong black woman and your strength in this ordeal will be an inspiration to thousands and tens of thousands around the country.

127

If there is anything that I can do, please do not hesitate to call. Or if you just want to call and talk, please do not hesitate to do that either.

May the peace and blessing Allah be upon you and your loved ones. Our prayers are with you.

As Salaam Alaikum!
Your Brother and Servant,
Minister Conrad Muhammad
New York Representative of
The Honorable Louis Farrakhan
And the Nation of Islam

RAE'S RAYS
© By Maxine L. Bryant

Rae
A name she calls herself.
Rae.
A drop of Golden Sun.
Who is this Rae that brings a breath
Of light to everyone she meets?
There is a saying, "To know me is to
Love me".
Not so with Rae.
To merely meet her is to love her.
Rae.
A narrow beam of light.
Rae.
A stream of electricity.
Yes. This is quite an accurate descriptive
Word for Rae.
For she electrifies everyone who come into her
presence.
She Rae-D-Ates a beam of hope to all who would
Otherwise choose despair.
She breath life to the dying,
Hope to the hopeless
And sight to the blind.
Rae.
A faint gleam.
Rae.
A burst of energy.
Those who've heard of her would
Expect one who's light is dimming.

Those who don't know her would
Suspect her to be weak.
Not so.
She Rae-D-Ates beauty to all.
She projects to all who would
Otherwise choose weakness.
I saw Rae once.
She dispersed light to my blinded eyes.
I spoke with Rae once.
She brightened my world with her words.
I touched Rae once.
She reached out and strengthened me with her
ray of hope.
Rae.
A thin line emerging from the center of
everything
Rae.
A very Special Lady.
To you, Rae Lewis-Thornton.
May God Bless You.

Dear Rae,

My name is Cynthia. I hope you don't mind being called by your first name. It's just that I feel as if I know you. Call me Cie (see).

When I saw your story on Nightline a couple of weeks ago, I was deeply moved. It inspired me to write the enclosed poem. My goal was to locate you and send this poem. I hope it finds you in good spirits and health. You are blessed to have someone dedicated to being by your side (of course you already know that). On another note, the world is certainly a better place with you in it. I would consider it an honor if you would call or write to let me know that my poem reached your hands. Rest assured you have made an eternal footprint in the sands of time.

*Take care of yourself
& God Bless!*

*Sincerely,
Cie*

Ode To Rae
Dedicated to Rae Lewis Thornton

You take each day
with dignified grace
Anguish hides beneath
A glowing face

Words of wisdom
Fall on eager ears
My pained heart cries
Out with silent cheers

You give of yourself
Amidst the strife –
A conscious choice
To celebrate life

To display courage
Extraordinaire...
To boldly fight
Because you care...

Bow at center stage
For your pursuit
Hats off to you
In heartfelt salute.

© Cynthia E. Holloway

United States Senate
Washington, DC 20510-1302

June 20, 1995
Dictated 6-19-95

Rae Lewis-Thornton
Contributing Editor
WBBM-CBS, Channel 2
630 North McClurg Court
Chicago, IL 60611

Dear Friend:

Just a note to say that I read the story in the <u>Chicago Tribune</u>, and it is an inspiring one. We're proud of you.

Sincerely,
Paul Simon
U. S. Senator

You talking about surprised, this note left me speechless! The fact that my U.S. Senator took the time to dictate a note to me was an honor. The fact that he read my story was a greater honor.

Senator Simon passed in December 2003, while this book was being edited. I had decided to add this letter prior to his death because I felt that it was awesome to be recognized for my efforts by my Senator. What a heroic of a man.

PART FOUR

A Circle of Friends

REFLECTION: A CIRLCE OF FRIENDS

$\mathcal{I}$ could not end this journey without including these few letters from my friends. Many people know that my support system is made up primarily of friends. And I have spoken often about my dysfunctional childhood in my speaking engagements. Sometimes families are not capable of giving you those things to sustain you, but I know first hand that God always fills the void.

Looking through my personal letters forced me to reflect on my life and those who provide me with the necessary love and support to cope with HIV. My step-grandmother (mama) who was the only mother I knew for the first eighteen years of my life, made her transition in August 2002. I never realized how permanent death really is until she made her transition. I guess you could say that mama was not a "core" part of my support system. She did not know how to be supportive. Mama knew what she knew...nothing more...nothing less... and that was that. But now that she is no longer here, there is a void. If I admit it to myself, there was a comfort in knowing that my mama was there. And if I am really honest, in the trenches, her home was my home. Now home was not always pleasant, but it was still home.

My biological family consist of a mother who loves me, but is emotionally paralyzed by past years of drug addiction; a grandmother, an aunt and 2 cousins, (whom I have never met) paralyzed by time, race and the fear of the unknown. My father made his transition when I was three years old. And his father, my grandfather who was my primary guardian, made his transition when I was 6 years old.

My support system consists' of people I have met on my life's journey. Overall, they do provide me with the necessary support that is required for someone living with a long-term illness. While I do have support, sometimes there are voids. I think in many ways it is easier to support someone whose illness is short-term and clear-cut, e.g. cancer. AIDS is murky. I do not look or act sick, so people stay in a self–induced denial. "She cannot really be that sick, she looks great. Look how she is traveling and going to school, I wish I had that kind of energy." I hear this all the time. I could be in the hospital bed sick beyond belief and people see what they want to see. Yes, it is a blessing that my physical appearance has not changed. Except with weight, too fat or too skinny, I still look pretty good. Just recently, I saw a friend and he asked in the course of the conversation, "You still sick?" Now, that was a revelation. My physical appearance, keeps my support system unbalanced.

I have also found that no one person can give all the support or even the same kind of support. You have to accept people's strengths and their weaknesses. In the end, you accept people where they are; sort of like them accepting me with HIV. As a result, I am never surprised by who shows up at the hospital to sit with me, who shows up at the house to cook a meal or just to drop one off or who does not. I have had disappointments equal to surprises. I have learned to have little expectations, just accept what people can and are willing to give. It is a vulnerable place. This is especially true for me because I do not have a traditional family support system.

I must admit, some have hung in better than others. Maybe everyone is not supposed to be with you on the entire journey. Some are there only for a season. As I was looking through my personal letters, it became clear that this section is only a reflection of who writes. There are many in my circle of friends that just do not write letters. This I must admit made me a little nervous, because everyone wants to be validated. So I thought I would introduce you to just some of the people in my life who do not write letters.

Missing from the pages are my "Young Ladies." Well, I met them all at different times and places in my journey. I have a very different relationship with each of them and yet I love them equally. They have truly been the core of my support system. They see what many others do not. They clean my house, wash my body when I am too sick or too weak to do it for myself, walk and baby-sit my dogs, and keep me laughing. But mostly, they help to keep me together. Sometimes, I am afraid that it is too much. I pray for their strength, I am grateful for their presence in my life. I met Toi, Davita, Ghemilia and Jenale' (Starr) ten years ago when I spoke at their high school, Hyde Park Career Academy in Chicago. Likewise, I met LaShonda when I spoke at her high school, Currie. Taisha, Chenne' and Johndalyn, I met through Davita. Aneysia came with Ghemilia and Loreal came with LaShonda. Tyanna, I met solo and Jayson came along. Shawnice, I have known since my days working at Operation PUSH and Nafeteria came with Shawnice. They each contribute to my life in different ways, but for sure they are my core.

Keith has never written, but he has certainly called from Zimbabwe, India, Ghana and many other far away places. He has truly been a friend. We go back to my political days. Many friends made a commitment when I first went public with my illness, but Keith was the one to keep it in every possible way. Core' is my oldest and dearest friend. She has been my rock for 26 years. She has been the one to hold my hand in my darkest moments with HIV and throughout my life. I will always be grateful for her friendship. Hazel (Nana) has been one of my biggest cheerleaders and my unpaid publicist. Leslie, Peter, Leo, Glenn and Cornell are my brother's beloved. Deidra is my kindred spirit. We are always

137

connected. She knows when things are not right and finds a way to lift me when I am down. She always has my back. Monika's my comfort. Ella, my Soror, is a God sent, she came into my life at the perfect time. She provides me with an unconditional ear. Henrietta's a blessing. Judy and Elmore are a gift from God. I met them eight years ago when I spoke at their church. They have provided unconditional support in my personal life and in my ministry. Karen keeps me level headed in the chaos of HIV. Ed Smith got back in the trenches. Mardge Cohen, my doctor, who has become my friend, helps to keep me alive. Dr. Greg helps to keep me emotionally and mentally stable.

Imani and Nambi, my Apricot Toy Poodles, bring me the most joy of them all. They are truly a blessing. No matter what, they are always there with the most unconditional love one could ever hope for. Those girls are special. When I am sick, they stay by my side. Funny, when I cry, they climb on me and try to stop me, by licking my tears. I truly could not imagine what my life would be without this little duo. I think they feel the same way. You know the statistics do show that people with long-term illness live longer when they have pets. They are truly my medicine.

Then there are those who are just a phone call away: Sandi and Jesse, Reverend and Mrs. Jesse Jackson, Rhoda, Georgette and Dr. Finney. Myra, Dwane, Audrey and Atha, Ruth and family, Reggie, Sanricka, Leslie and Mike, Donna and Delvin, Tracey, Pastor Charles Jenkins and Reverend Clay Evans, and all the ladies of Delta Sigma Theta Sorority, Inc. Now, meet some of my circle of friends through their letters.

Barry Saunders was one of my closest friends on the planet. We met back in 1985 at the Congressional Black Caucus. Of course, Barry being the man that he was "hit on me." But I was not interested. Not that he was not worthy, I am sure that there are many that can attest to that, but I was dating someone and wanted to be faithful. Overtime, Barry endeared himself to me. He had that kind of personality. This was especially true when it came to women. At his funeral "his women" were there, "Representing!" Most of us did not date him. He was our friend and he made each of us feel special. We all could claim and did, that we had a special place in his heart and for the most part, we all accepted each other, with only mild jealousy. That was Barry.

He was one of the first five to know my HIV status. In those early days, he held my hand and kept my secret. I remember when the *Essence* article was published, his current girlfriend who never believed that Barry and I were "just friends" put his back against the wall. He assured her, that we had never "gone there" and that my HIV status was none of her business. We were truly friends.

He gave me away at my wedding and got people straight when they dared to talk about me getting married with AIDS. Even though he supported my marriage, he was the first to tell me to leave that man and to cut my losses when the marriage became unhealthy. He threatened to come to Chicago many days to get things straight. Make no mistakes, he had my back. That was Barry.

Our friendship was a little strained after I wrecked his BMW driving from North Carolina to Washington D.C. He had driven to North Carolina to hear me speak. On the way back, while I was driving in a drenching rainstorm, the woman ahead of me stopped in the middle of the freeway, visibility was impossible. The long and short of it, I hit her. Boy, her car did not have a scratch, but Barry's car was totaled. My insurance paid the bill, but for a while, things were a little tense.

We often joked that our lives were parallel. We both worked in politics for basically the same people. And it seems like our dating habits were similar, when I dated someone ten years older than me, he dated someone ten years older.

He was my hero. He told me often, that I was his hero. But truly, he had more guts than I think I could ever have. Barry was diagnosed with cancer of the tongue. He chose an experimental surgery where they removed 75% of his tongue. The doctors told him that he probably would not survive, or if he did, he would never talk again. Not true. That was another thing that we had in common, a long-term illness. But the one thing that really binds us was our faith. He survived and talked.

Barry had courage. He could no longer eat solid foods after the surgery, but that did not stop him. It was the most humbling experience for me to see a man, who loved to eat soul food, prepare meals of ensure, oatmeal and melted ice cream. He was my hero. In spite of his challenges, he never wavered or faltered on friendship. When Barry was your friend, you had a friend for life. The same was also true if you were his enemy.

When I was sick, Barry would fly to Chicago for a day to check on me. He never let me go hungry or broke. The stability of my finances has and remains an

140

issue. When I am not speaking, there is no income. All I had to say to Barry was that I had no speaking engagements for the month; money would be in the mail. I never had to ask. I say often that proud people never ask, he made sure that I remained proud.

There is so much that I can say about Barry. Seven years after his first surgery from the mouth cancer, he was diagnosed with bilateral lung cancer. This boy did chemotherapy and never missed a day of work. His strength was always an encouragement to my spirit. He never asked God why me? You see Barry never smoked a cigarette a day in his life. He accepted his plight to the very end. He never gave into the darkness. His life inspires me to never give up. Like Barry, I want to keep on going and see what the end is going to be. When I eventually make my transition, I pray that I do it with the same grace and dignity that Barry exhibited during his entire illness. I know that he is in heaven holding court, getting them ready, cause we are one awesome team.

Oh, I miss him. Some days I say, I need to call Barry. Then I remember, he made his transition January 26, 2001. Barry was one of my biggest cheerleaders. I know that he is "up there" rooting for me. He believed in my ministry. This is one of the notes that he sent me on my birthday.

To my sister,

You are a very special person to all but especially to me. Your friendship has impacted me profoundly and through my life, you touched others.

I'm reminded of the expressions that says, "I'm not at this point in life because who I am but because whose I am." You truly are a child of God and his love shines through you always.

As you move through life just remember you have the strength we have the love.

As Always...
With Love,
Barry

Taisha is the teenager in the group of "Young Ladies" who have become my family. I met her about eight years ago through Davtia. I have watched her grow and mature into a wonderful young lady with a promising future. I am glad she is a part of my life. In her own way, she is a quite storm in my life. I could not imagine what my life would be without her, she definitely adds to the circle. This paper that she wrote while in the 8th grade, on "Women In History," really surprised me. I had no idea that I had touched her life in this way. This paper has been a highlight in my life. Might I add, she got an A. I was really touched.

Women In History

Women have made many significant contributions to our society. Without a doubt, the United States of America would not be the strongest nation in the world were it not for the accomplishments of many strong women. Women have invented, created and developed many things in our communities. We should honor these visionaries for making society better in every way. For a long time, women were not recognized for their diligence and fortitude. So, March should be their time to 'shine' for all the work and good things that they have done.

Several women have contributed tremendously to the world. Madam C.J. Walker invented hair care products for people to use. Mrs. Pasteur helped to invent the pasteurization process so that milk would not spoil so quickly. A woman,

143

Catherine Littlefield-Green, actually invented the cotton gin and many other things but because women were not readily given patents, Eli Whitney was given the credit for the invention. Times have certainly changed, now women can invent spectacular things and get credit for them and get credit for them without having to go through sexist and discriminatory red tape and bureaucracy.

My aunt, Ms. Rae Lewis-Thornton is a woman who I feel is a role model. She is a world renowned A.I.D.S., activist. She is living with this deadly disease, and fortunately at this moment she is extremely healthy. She has been on dozens of nationally syndicated televisions shows, radio shows, and speaking engagements telling people her story. She does this to raise awareness and hopes that no one else will contract the H.I.V. virus. In addition to that, my Aunt is currently a Reverend at a famous and historical Baptist Church and she is in seminary working on a degree in divinity. Despite this very hectic schedule she still finds time to give motivational and inspirational speeches on how the A.I.D.S. disease has affected her life. She does not live her life in shame, nor does she feel sorry for herself. She has used this tough situation to make her stronger. Her courage is the character trait that I think makes her a great role model.

I can honestly say that my Aunt has helped shape my life greatly. She's taught me how to act like I have a strong sense of right and wrong and good moral character. She has shown me that there are consequences for every behavior and that I should make wise choices. Moreover, she has also shown me that I can make the best out of an adverse situation and come out on top of it. One of the most important lessons that she has shared with me is that, it is important to be not only book smart but street smart as well. I love, respect, and admire my aunt because she is courageous, ambitious and selfless.

Rae Lewis-Thornton should receive the Woman in History award because she is a fine example of what one can achieve if we only believe in ourselves. She is constantly working to prevent what happened to her from happening to others. She has found the courage to rise above her situation and not use it as an excuse. She is not dying from a deadly disease; she has learned to live with it. Despite all of that, she juggles a busy schedule between an A.I.D.S. activist, a minister, a student, and fantastic Aunt. These are only a few of the reasons why Rae Lewis-Thornton should be recognized as a powerful living legend. Wouldn't you agree?

Tyanna is my Soror and another one of my "Young Ladies" and the newest to the gang. I met her when I spoke at her school, the University of Iowa, almost two years ago. She had just graduated in December and came right back in January just to hear me speak. After the speaking engagement, as typical of me, I had dinner with the collegiate Sorors of my wonderful sorority Delta Sigma Theta. Tyanna and I ended up at the same end of the table; we started talking and one thing led to another. There was something about her spirit. Before I knew it, I had offered her a part-time job to tie her over until a "real" one came through. She has become a major contributor to my support system. I think that sometimes people fail to realize that when I am too sick to clean the house and go grocery shopping, those things still need to happen. It takes many to support one. No one person can do it. She just slid right on in. The rest of the gang feels as if she has always been around. She has risen to the occasion as a sister in Christ and as a Soror.

Dear Rae,

Thank you for giving me the opportunity to work by your side. It was an honor to work for my role model, which just happens to be an honorary member of such a noteworthy organization. You wear so may hats in my eyes: role model, mentor, soror, and sister in Christ. I wish you the very best in all of your endeavors and pray your ministry reaches heights you couldn't even imagine. I love you and God Bless.

Soror

Toi Salter is definitely a woman who practices her faith. She has truly been a friend. I first met her in the Cheesecake Factory in 1994. She approached me and asked if I was the woman who was on the cover of *Essence*. We struck up a conversation. For years, I would see her out and about. (The diva socialite that she is). We would always strike up a conversation and promise to get together. It did not happen until almost two years ago. She saw me in Saks. I was shoe shopping until I dropped. Along with another Diva Sister and friend Allison Payne, they invited me to lunch; it lasted well into the dinner hour. The rest has been history. Toi recognized that my support system was small. Yeah, I know a lot of people, but knowing people does not make a support system.

Back to Toi. This diva has cooked me meals when I was too sick to cook myself; kept me in prayer; been a source of constant encouragement in some of my darkest moments and made sure that I had more than $58.00 in the bank in my lowest financial times. She is truly a woman of her word. She had kept the promises made to me in this note after her birthday party two years ago. I am grateful that God sent her my way. Just knowing her has enriched my life. She is indeed the Christian Woman she professes. She is all that, plus a bag of chip and a mystic, and of course wearing Escada.

Rae,

What a true blessing it is to know you with your uplifting and radiant spirit. I'm glad that we ran into each other in Saks - actually that was probably divine intervention. Thanks so much for your generosity on my birthday. I love my Tiffany cross and my Jabez book. Rae, as much support that you give everyone else in your career and life, I want you to know that I am here for you as a friend as well as others and we're here for the long haul. My God continue to bless and keep you.

Love,
Toi

As I was plowing through the hundreds of letters that I have received over the years, this particular letter took me by total surprise. I had even forgotten that she had sent it. It is amazing to me how God works. Some people call it luck. Reverend Jeanne and I would certainly say that it was the Holy Spirit moving.

Almost six years after our first meeting and this letter, our paths crossed at McCormick Theological Seminary. I was in my second year in the Master of Divinity program when Jeanne came to McCormick for the same program. She reminded me who she was, but of course it took me weeks to really connect the dots. The cat is out of the bag. Yes, I sort of forgot. I have met so many people, it is hard to keep track. This is especially true with diarrhea, fatigue, a pill load of 26 a day and a crazy back breaking schedule that I must maintain.

One day, Jeanne saw me in the hallway just before class. It was one of those challenging days of being my mother's caregiver. (Mama was in her second year of inoperable mouth cancer. A place that neither of us would have believed it so.) Jeanne picked up on my broken spirit. Mama had not been nice that day.

Jeanne approached me and began to minister! The rest is history. She has truly become my sister beloved. Our time together at McCormick will always be cherished. We had many "debriefings." Staying true to ones theology is critical in ministry. You need to know what you believe and why. So we held each others hand, as we stayed true to our beliefs.

Our friendship is truly a testament to the work of the Holy Spirit, which moves in the lives of people. My ministry was a blessing to her. Look how God works. Her ministry has become a blessing to me.

Dear Rae:

This is just a little note to let you know that you have stayed on my mind since I met you on Dr. Finney's T.V. Show. My name is Jeanne and you and I and Madelyn (the make-up artist) talked at length and then prayed together.

I've been praying for you, asking God to give you strength... especially to go through the doors that He is opening for you.

Your words of wisdom on unconditional love touched me so much that I've continued to ponder upon that concept. I realize, though, the secret of unconditional love is to love. - to act on God's love and not just to ponder it.

To that end the Lord laid you on my heart to show a small token of love. Enclosed please find 2 tickets to our women's fellowship luncheon and reception on Saturday, Sept 21. It's sponsored by the women of the Apostolic Church of God. If you are able to come, I'd love for you to be my guest. Feel free to call me if you have any questions.

Again, Thank God for you.
Agape'
Jeanne

This is only one of the many letters of encouragement that I have received from Erika since I met her after speaking at Northern Illinois University where she attended, well over seven years ago. She has become a permanent fixture in my life. She is one of my "Young Ladies," of whom I am very proud.

Dear Rae,

I pray that this letter reaches you in good spirits. As always you are on my mind and in my prayers. I pray for the growth of your ministry, your impact on people, and your strength to continue to save the lives of others, your physical strength and I thank God for the invaluable lesson that you have taught me. That is WHEN LIFE GIVES YOU LEMONS, MAKE LEMONADE!!! This is key in survival. You are the definition of strength and beauty. I admire you most of your dedication to education and your willingness to do God's will. You are blessed and if I can be 1/10 of a role model as you in my lifetime I will be honored. You are most deserving of His abundant life and I will continue to support you. Thank you for taking the time to know me and always remember that I am available to you if you need me.

Love your friend,
Erika

I met Reverend Bill only a couple of years after I was diagnosed with HIV, which makes him one of those very few who knew my status early and supported me. Over the years, he has given me both unconditional friendship and unconditional love. For this, I will be eternally grateful. Not only does he provide moral support, he has also supported my ministry. He was one of my first friends to bring me to speak. In fact, he organized a World AIDS Day program in his hometown December 1, 1994, the day that the *Essence* article hit the newsstand. I received this particular letter a couple of years ago after a speaking engagement in his area. This letter was only a reminder of his support for my ministry and of me. I am glad to call him my friend. I know that his love will never falter.

My Dearest Rae,

As has been the case since I noticed you across a crowded room, God's print of uniqueness and anointing rest upon you.

Since indeed what comes from the heart touches the heart, as the message was filled with principles that point to inner and emotional prosperity. It is through our trials and test that our faith is fortified!

Stay focused and faithful; your best is yet to be.

Until we meet, Bill

* * *

Since being inducted into Delta Sigma Theta Sorority, Inc. I have spoken for many Delta chapters both collegiate and alumnae. I say often, it is good to be a Delta. This is especially true for me because I grew-up in an environment that was unkind. I was told many days, as a young girl, that I would never be "nothing." My family wrote me off, but God saw fit to write me into history, Delta's history. It is awesome that my name is placed in a category with other incredible African-American Women such as Fannie Lou Hamer, Mary Church Terrell, Nikki Giovanni, Lena Horne and Mary McLeod Bethune, just to name a few.

As a tribute to my sorority, I included just some of the letters that I have received from my Sorors since my induction in Chicago in 2000. I am proud of my sorority, not only have they brought me to speak and lifted-up my ministry, but also, HIV/AIDS has continually been a national focus for our sorority. I honor their work around HIV and I thank God that they honor my ministry. It is good to be a Delta.

Your Soror,
Rae Lewis-Thornton
2000/Grand Chapter

Soror Thornton,

You were an absolute joy! Everything antici-pated and more! Our prayers go with you as you continue to fulfill God's purpose for your life.

In Delta Love,
Lambda Theta
University of Alabama

Soror Rae Lewis-Thornton,

On behalf of the Lambda Kappa Chapter of Delta Sigma Theta Sorority, Inc., we just wanted to thank you for sharing with us your motive-tional words. You are truly an inspiration to us all. We are so proud to have you as a soror! However, you are not only a phenomenal soror you are also a phenomenal woman and human being. God bless you, and may you continue to spread your words to educate and enlighten us all. We hope to see you again soon, Soror!

Yours in Delta,
Yakini Mack-Williams
Vice President and Alisa Reese
President
University of Maryland-Baltimore, Co
We love you, Soror!

Dearest Soror,

I have been blessed twice this year being able to see and hear your powerful message. Soror Thornton from the moment I heard your story in my University 101 book, I have been truly inspired. It is wonderful that things worked out in our favor and you were able to join us today. You are such a dynamic and powerful woman in every way possible. You are truly my hero and it is wonderful to see you again. Beautiful, poised, confidant, and an exemplary...you are a teacher and a mentor to us all. Soror, you are loved and appreciated for all that you do day to day.

Thanks again,
Kelli Anderson
Hampton University

Soror,

On behalf of Delta Sigma Theta Sorority, Inc. Eta Kappa Chapter, we would like to thank you for your presence here today. Your testimony is an inspiration and exemplification of the perfection we all try to achieve. In the spirit of our founders who began our legacy of excellence and service, we are proud to be called your sorors and glad that you are able to impact and influence our Spellman sisters. We love you and again we thank you!!!

Delta Sigma Theta Sorority, Inc.
Eta Kappa Chapter

Greetings Soror,

Thanks for all you have done. Theta Alpha truly appreciates you! Look for a violet soon!

Sincerely yours,
Theta Alpha

Soror Thornton,

Thank you for simply sharing your story. I pray that you are doing much better than you were on Sunday evening and that you were able to complete your class assignment. You've touched the lives of many and you're nothing short of a blessing. I've been thinking of many things you said on Sunday night and simply can't get them out of my mind. During your talk, you spoke of all the tangible things you possess, but they don't matter because just as surely as you stood you were dying, we all are! We've all come to fulfill a purpose then these old bodies fade away—but our spirit lives forever. Do know, unlike the 19 year-old pregnant girl w/AIDS, somebody in the place will make your story applicable to their own lives. Know that your living is _not_ in vain.

In our Founders love,
LaTasha L. Cain
University of Illinois-Champaign-Urbana

A Tribute to Rae

Sometimes as you walk thru life,
You may receive a heavy blow
It may not knock you down
But your progress becomes
A little slow
This is the time when God is testing your faith:
You can choose to fold
Or in charge of your destiny, you can take...
A different path.
Letting your light shine thru
As a guide for others,
You become, a strong, voice
You teach and inspire
You turn and tragedy into a triumph

Montgomery
Alpha XI Chapter
Delta Sigma Theta Sorority, Inc.

Aneysia is the youngest of my "Young Ladies." At age 5, she is sometimes the wisest. They say, "From the mouth of babes."

Every Wednesday is our day. I pick her up from school and take her to ballet class. On the way, we have tea and a lively conversation. When ballet is over, we come home and I make dinner while she is playing with Imani. Sometimes, we "rock and roll," her words, and paint or color. We do other things too, like go to the museum and the zoo.

She makes me happy. Occasionally, she will catch me taking my medication. Her eyes get big (I take 26 pills a day). I explain to her that Auntie Rae has an "owie." I ask her to pray that I get better, and she does.

I hope and pray that I live long enough for her to understand. I am blessed because she is in my circle. This is one of the letters she wrote to me one day after ballet class. Of course, she asked me how to spell most of the words.

Love

Thank You For Ballet
I Love You
Auntie Rae

Aneysia

Amazing

Grace

Letters Along My Journey

Please visit website:
www.raelewisthornton.org

To order copies of Amazing Grace:
Rae Lewis-Thornton, Inc.
1507 East 53rd Street
Suite 315
Chicago, IL 60615

ISBN 0-9747983-0-4

Please make checks payable to Rae Lewis-Thornton, Inc.

Ship to:
Name _____
Address _____
City _____
State/Zip _____

Quantity   _____
Book Total $ _____
Postage & Handling $ _____
Total Amount Due $ _____